9⁷⁵

PASTOR
AS
PERSON

Faith Hardy Christians

D1022793

PASTOR AS PERSON

GARY L. HARBAUGH

AUGSBURG Publishing House • Minneapolis

PASTOR AS PERSON

Copyright © 1984 Augsburg Publishing House

All rights reserved. Except for brief quotations in critical articles or reviews, no part of this book may be reproduced in any manner without prior written permission from the publisher. Write to: Permissions, Augsburg Publishing House, 426 S. Fifth St., Box 1209, Minneapolis MN 55440.

Scripture quotations unless otherwise noted are from the Revised Standard Version of the Bible, copyright 1946, 1952, and 1971 by the Division of Christian Education of the National Council of Churches.

Library of Congress Cataloging in Publication Data

Harbaugh, Gary L., 1936-
  PASTOR AS PERSON.

  Bibliography: p.
  1. Clergy—Office.   2. Clergy—Psychology.
I. Title.
BV660.2.H3158 1984   253′.2   84-24259
ISBN 0-8066-2115-X (pbk.)

Manufactured in the U.S.A.   APH 10-4889

         3   4   5   6   7   8   9   0   1   2   3   4   5   6   7   8   9

Contents

Acknowledgments

The writing of a book requires many gifts, all of them from God, but most of them experienced through other people. At two turning points in my life, the work of Paul Tournier and the personal support of Elisabeth Kübler-Ross helped me to gain perspective on what it means to be a person. Richard C.W. Hall and Robert Plutchik have given me encouragement and example. Bishop Kenneth H. Sauer, T. A. Kantonen, and Frank H. Seilhamer have given me the gifts of inspiration and affirmation. Fred W. Meuser, James M. Childs Jr., Linda Ault, and Eugene R. Dahnke have given me collegial blessing, released time, and research assistance. The Aid Association for Lutherans and Lutheran Brotherhood have supported my studies, and the staff of Augsburg Publishing House has given me the advantage of an editorial perspective. The greatest gifts have been that of acceptance and understanding from those who best know this pastor as a person: Marlene, Cary, Heidi, Joel, Tracy, and Chris.

Preface

Pastors are persons. Most of the problems pastors experience in the parish are not caused by the pastor forgetting he or she is a pastor. Most difficulties pastors face in the parish arise when the pastor forgets that he or she is a person.

This book is about the pastor as a person. It is a book about the experience of people who are pastors—their thoughts and feelings and behaviors. But this is also a reflective book, bringing to bear upon the pastors and their situations the perspectives of anthropology, the behavioral sciences, and philosophy, as well as theology.

The pastor is not only a person; he or she is a *whole* person, a whole person in Christ.[1] In Chapter 1 I will introduce you to some pastors. Then, with their help, I will share with you the (w)holistic* model that underlies my research and reflection on the person of the pastor. This model will acquaint you with most of my assumptions.

---

*The (w)holistic model employed in this book is a biblically based concept that incorporates elements from other wholistic and holistic literature. The use of parentheses in the spelling of the term will indicate the places where I am specifically referring to my own model.

The (w)holistic model will also help you understand the progression of the subsequent chapters. The model identifies the four dimensions of our humanness: the physical, mental, emotional, and social, and their integration in the spiritual. In the following chapters, each of these four dimensions is presented, one at a time, in relation to a common pastoral "problem." For example, Chapter 2 looks at the pastor as a physical person, an embodied being. With the body as the focus, the problem of pastoral stress and burnout is presented in relation to the experiences of Pastor Tom Daniels.*

After each of the four case studies, I invite you to reflect on the identified problem from a variety of points of view. In Chapter 2, for instance, stress is explored from biological, psychological, and sociological perspectives.

Finally, in each chapter I suggest that the identified pastoral problem is not only a threat to the pastor as a person, but also a challenge. Relevant questions are raised that will be readdressed in the concluding chapter on integration.

The "problems" identified are major concerns for those in ordained ministry. In Chapter 3 we look at the pastor as a *thinking* person. The problem for the pastor is how to maintain a good and faithful balance between filling the pastoral role and living a healthy, happy personal life. Pastor Joan Russell's story not only illustrates the problem, but also enables us to see how seminary education can contribute to the difficulties many pastors experience in this area.

Chapter 4 follows the *feelings* of Pastor John Jeffrich as he faces loss. The pastor often functions as a central, comforting figure in the grief situations of others. John's story provides an opportunity for us to look at how a pastor handles his own grief responses as he deals with the diversity of loss situations in the parish.

Pastor Chris's anger is a point of connection between the pastor as a feeling person and the pastor as a *relating* person, the focus of Chapter 5. Since Chris's interpersonal problems extend beyond the parish to the parsonage, his case provides us with an opportunity to discuss clergy conflicts from a variety of viewpoints.

In Chapter 6 the problems of stress, the tension between person and role, personal loss in the parish, and interpersonal conflict are reviewed from the perspectives of the *risks* of choice and the *potential* inherent in those choices for integration as a whole person. I suggest that the pastor's personal choices and the way those choices are made provide the most powerful "proclamation" we can offer in our ministry as a person in Christ.

My approach is experiential and open-ended. I begin with the life experiences of pastoral persons, reflect on that experience from secular as well as religious perspectives, and raise questions and make suggestions that point toward integrative action as a whole person in Christ.[2]

I believe that we who are in Christ are able to learn from our life experiences in a special way. The gospel tells me that I am chosen, known, and loved. There is nothing I can learn about myself that God does not already know, and still I am loved. This gives me courage to open myself to any perspective that promises to help me better understand myself and my experiences.

Pastors want both their professional and personal lives to reflect God's new creation in Christ. But things get in our way. To live life as a grace-full gift may require that we look at some familiar problems in a fresh way—then *do* something about what we see.

This book is intended to help the pastor consider taking some personal steps that could be life-changing. At times we know something must be done, but we are not certain what. When you read about the experiences of Tom, Joan, John, and Chris you may get some ideas. But you still have to decide what is the best and most faithful next step for you. When we have considered as carefully and prayerfully as we can, Luther's counsel is for us to "sin boldly." Luther realized that sin darkens our decisions. But there comes a time when we must act on the basis of what light we have, trusting that we are truly acceptable to God through Christ.

Grace gives us the courage to take decisive action. Grace also reminds us, even as we act, to remain open to other possibilities. The final word is never our own. It belongs to God.

---

* Except for the author's references to himself, no name or situation in this book reflects a particular individual, and none should be inferred. The main *themes*, however, have appeared repeatedly in the author's research, and in that sense the stories are true-to-life.

The Pastor as Person: A (W)holistic Model

When Tom Daniels* opened the letter from his old seminary, he thought it would just be another request for support. Instead, Tom learned that the seminary was planning to introduce a course called "The Person in Ministry." The course would be scheduled during a student's first term and was a response, in part, to the changing patterns of enrollment. With increasing numbers of women and second-career students interested in ordained ministry, the seminary thought that an introductory course that focused on the pastor as a person might be helpful. Tom was one of a randomly selected group of experienced pastors who were being asked to offer some suggestions on how best to approach the course. To keep the study from being too narrow, the seminary also suggested that the question might be raised at Tom's local ministerial association.

Interested in just about everything and eager to lend a hand, Tom was excited about receiving the letter. He also felt that, after his years in the parish, he had some ideas about seminary education, but he had never before been asked to offer them. The topic was meaningful, too, because Tom had never been so aware of himself as a person. Since he had turned 40, and especially since coming to Messiah congregation, Tom had found that his long-established way of going about his ministry was becoming in-

* See the note at the bottom of p. 11.

creasingly difficult. The energy just was not there as it once had been. As a matter of fact, Tom planned to see his physician right after the ministerial meeting.

Having a meeting was Tom's idea. There was no active ministerial association in his community, but Tom thought it would be good to get some ideas from some of the other ministers in town. He and four other pastors had planned a joint Easter sunrise service last year and, when he called them, they were all interested in offering some suggestions. Joan Russell, pastor of the First Community Church, was the only female and the youngest pastor in the community, except perhaps for Paul Denning, the assistant at St. Peter's. Chris Campbell was the senior pastor at St. Peter's, a large, prestigious church in the center of town. Chris was planning to retire in another year or so. The fourth colleague was John Jeffrich, the busy pastor of Good Shepherd, a bustling congregation, really too much for one pastor, although it did have an exceptional lay ministry.

Everyone except Paul Denning was present and on time. Tom had no way of knowing it, but each of the pastors who attended the meeting was privately dealing with a personal problem that related in one way or another to the seminary's question. Just before lunch, Joan had received a telephone call from a committee from St. James, a parish in another state where she had interned before she graduated from seminary. The chairman asked if she were available for a call to become pastor there. While Joan had not been at First Community Church very long, she had been going through a troubling internal struggle about whether or not the ordained ministry was really for her. She did not feel free to tell any of the other pastors in the community about her thoughts and feelings. Joan avoided giving an immediate response by telling the call committee she would get back to them around dinner time with an answer.

The other two pastors were similarly preoccupied with individual concerns. John Jeffrich had just come from a counseling session. He had not been able to shake the problems out of his mind. He knew that another appointment should have been made, but later in the afternoon he was to drive out of town with Ellen, his wife. Something had to be done about Ellen's grandmother, and Ellen's parents asked whether she and John could help with the decision. John was torn between his responsibility as a pastor and as a husband.

Chris Campbell was the last member of the committee who was able to come. His assistant, Paul, was out of town for the day. Chris had some questons about pastoral identity since Paul joined his staff, because Paul's approach to ministry was so different from his. Chris wondered whether maybe he had been a pastor too long and was somehow out of touch. Being so close to retirement, Chris had little incentive to change, but he felt he might have something to suggest to seminarians just beginning.

After spending a little time socializing over coffee and donuts, everyone seemed ready to get started and Tom opened the session with a brief reading from Scripture and a prayer for guidance. Tom began the discussion by reading the letter his seminary had sent. Then Tom invited the group to respond.

"The changes your seminary describes are taking place in our denomination as well," said Joan, "except we didn't have a course like you're planning. I think it's a good idea to look at the student as an individual, because some of the old seminary approaches just don't fit the new situation."

"Don't say 'old' to someone ready to retire," Chris chimed in, with a chuckle. "In many ways, I think ministers in my day had a much easier time. Everybody knew what it meant to be a preacher and there wasn't so much confusion as there is today. One of the things that occurs to me is that our idea of what it is to be a pastor changes over the years. My pension board has been sending me a lot of literature on the life cycle. I think your seminary might give some real thought to approaching the person in ministry from that perspective."

"Thanks, Chris," said Tom. "That's a helpful suggestion. I find I'm a different person today than I was 20 years ago, too. My mind still goes like I'm 20, but my body has a hard time keeping up. Those changes do make a difference in my ministry. Does anyone else have another idea?"

"Well," John said, "I think it would be helpful for your seminary to start with what the Bible says not just about pastors but about *all* people, and then tie that into the present ministry situation. My denomination is doing a lot of study about what it means to be baptized into Christ and how that opens up the whole area of lay ministry. I hope your seminary won't think about a person in ministry only as being in *ordained* ministry."

"That's a good point," Tom said. "Most of the people who go to my seminary do go into ordained ministry, but there are several lay ministry programs, too. Personally, I was wondering if any of you agree that another approach to a course like this is to see the pastor in relation to the parish situation. What is going on in a parish has a lot of effect on us."

"I say amen to that," John responded quickly. "Just before this meeting I was talking with a woman who was wondering what to do about her daughter. Probably not a lot can be done as long as the situation at home is so bad. I think the same thing is true for pastors. I don't mean home life, necessarily, but certainly the parish. A pastor is really affected by his, excuse me Joan, his or her parish situation. A lot of personal identity comes from the environment, and I think this is true for pastors, too."

"You're right," Joan jumped in, "but I also think something needs to be said about personal responsibility. One of the hardest things that I've found as a new pastor is to make major decisions that affect so many people. I never had much help in seminary with that. In fact, after being in the seminary a little while, some seminarians have to decide whether or not to stay. For some, it's a real faith crisis. One of my friends really had a tough time with that."

The group then discussed some experiences of themselves and their friends in theological school. After a while, Tom looked at his watch and realized he would have to rush to get to his doctor's office on time. "OK," Tom said. "This has really been helpful. We've come up with a lot of ideas, maybe too many for one course, unless the seminary finds some way to tie them together. I'll send in a summary of our discussion and see what happens."

Tom left to make his appointment with his physician, and John left to pick up Ellen. Joan went back to her office to think about how she was going to respond to the call committee, and Chris left to meet with Ann Richards, who had telephoned and said she needed to see him as soon as possible.

The ministerial meeting had gone quite well. Tom's colleagues identified resources and perspectives each of which has something important to say about the person in ministry. Few pastors would argue with John that the Bible is basic and a good place to start. However, we can infer from their discussion that this group believes psychology and a number of other disciplines also have valuable contributions to make. Since they touched on physical and psychological as well as spiritual concerns, we can also infer that they are concerned about the *whole* person in ministry.

The new course on the person in ministry might encourage seminarians to think about themselves as persons, not just from the psychological perspective, but also from the standpoint of the Bible. A review of what the Bible says about persons would bring to the seminarian a renewed sense of being part of the people of God in history—the history of the believing community and the personal history of the believer. This would enable the seminarian to move right into the area of Chris's concern, life-cycle theory. Developmental psychology helps us appreciate how our bodies and minds and hearts are shaped, in part, through the accumulated experiences of our past. And John's point about life situations is well taken, also. Current psychotherapies remind us that, as relating persons, we are affected by our interpersonal and wider social environment. Joan's intuition about decisions is equally insightful. Christian theology guides us to see how, as believing and valuing persons we bring our personal history and our life situation to integration in the choices we make. Each of the approaches suggested by the pastors' group makes a definite contribution to the understanding of the pastor as a person. Moreover, these points of view do not need to be considered independently of each other.

The purpose of this chapter is to develop an integrative model that will graphically depict the interrelationship and interaction of all of these perspectives on the person in ministry. Although much of what is discussed will be relevant to lay ministry, the primary focus will be on the pastor as a person. Chapters 2–6 will demonstrate how an integrative, (w)holistic model may be of help in a pastor's self-understanding as the pastor deals with the typical stresses of parish life. Before we turn to application in specific pastoral situations, however, we must more closely review the biblical, psychological, and theological foundations on which we shall develop our theme of the pastor as a person, a *whole* person, in Christ.

What the Bible Says about Personhood

The Bible tells us three things crucial to our understanding of the pastor as a person. First, the Bible is the basis of our understanding of a person as a whole person, an *irreducible* whole. Second, wholeness in the Bible is not solely a personal matter, as we might tend to think, influenced as we are by the individualism of contemporary society. In the biblical view personal wholeness can be understood only when an individual is seen in relationship with others. Finally, a person is truly whole only in relationship with God.

While most pastors would readily agree that the Bible supports a view of persons as whole persons, it is not always so clear that the Bible understands persons *only* as whole persons. Until the biblical scholarship of the twentieth century challenged the assumption, Christians for centuries did not question the Greek philosophical teaching that the body was separate from the soul.[3]

The Whole Person

A brief review of some basic biblical concepts will help us think our way back into the Hebrew and early Christian way of looking at persons as an indivisible whole.[4] The Hebrew word for soul (*nephesh*) is usually translated in the New Testament by the word *psyche*, which means "self," "mind," "personality," or "life." When we read in Genesis 2:7 (KJV) that "the Lord God formed man of the dust from the ground, and breathed into his nostrils the breath of life; and man became a living soul [*nephesh*]," it is clear that *nephesh* here indicates not a part, but the whole. Does one *have* a *nephesh*? That is not the biblical question. A human being *is* a living *nephesh*, gifted with life by God.

The biblical words for body and even parts of the body emphasize that same wholeness. While the word for flesh (Hebrew, *basar*, Greek, *sarx*) is used to show the unity of *all* creatures, the word for body (*soma*) denotes the person created by and for God. In the Bible, the body "often stands for the total personality of man just as 'the body of Christ' is the whole Christian church."[5] The evidence is strong enough for biblical scholars to state without equivocation, "The Hebrew idea of the personality is an animated body. . . . Man does not *have* a body, he *is* a body."[6]

The argument is no less compelling when it comes to parts of the body, such as the heart (Hebrew, *leb*; Greek, *kardia*). The Hebrews had no conception of physiology comparable to our own. Consequently, the Hebrew could say that a person's heart died within him, without literally meaning that the heart stopped beating (1 Sam. 25:37). Hebrew reference to bodily organs such as heart is usually figurative rather than literal. The heart was understood to be a center of emotions, although it could also be understood in relation to individual intellect or will. In repentance, a person could request a "new" or "clean" heart (Ps. 51:10; cf. Ezek. 36:26). God's response is to renew the whole person.

Jesus did not reject Hebrew anthropology, and neither did the early Christian church. In the Bible a person is understood to be whole and indivisible, a psychophysical unity.[7] While a person may be addressed in terms of his or her body, mind, emotions, or in a variety of other ways, when God or the believing community speaks, the appropriate response is that of the whole person with all our heart, soul, mind, and strength (Mark 12:29ff.).

The Whole Person in Relationship

The second emphasis of the Bible is that the whole person is always a person in relationship. As we noted, the individual is related to all other creatures, but especially to other persons. While individuality is highly prized today and only a few seem to have a social conscience, the biblical perspective on individuality always includes participation with the community. The Israelite person had identity only in relation to Israel, the people of God. Separation from the community was synonymous with disintegration, disease, and death. Hope and healing meant restoration to the community. The healed lepers were told, "Go and show yourselves to the priests" (Luke 17:14). Being in a right relationship with yourself meant being in a right relationship with the community. Scripture teaches us that the person becomes a person only in relation to other persons. Personal wholeness is inextricably involved with a person's interpersonal and social context.[8]

The Whole Person and God

When the Bible speaks of relationship, however, relationship is more than kinship with creation or other creatures. Biblical anthropology is (w)holistic in that the creature cannot be understood except in relation to the Creator. The Hebrew word *shalom* brings together the personal, interpersonal, and theological significance of wholeness by pointing to the internal, horizontal, and vertical dimensions of "peace." To have *shalom* is to be in right relationship with oneself, one's neighbor, and one's God. This is *life*, and anything short of this is, in the Hebrew — and Christian — perspective, a form of death.[9] The first and greatest commandment, Jesus told us, is to love the Lord our God wholeheartedly, and then our neighbor as ourself (Mark 12:29-31). The biblical view is of a person called to a life of love and peace with oneself, others, and God.

A Biblical Model of Wholeness

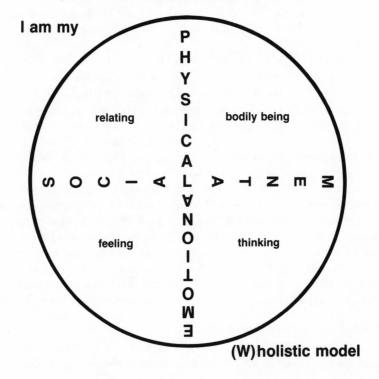

I am my

relating   bodily being

feeling   thinking

(W)holistic model

This (w)holistic model arranges the physical, mental, emotional, and social dimensions of humanness in such a way as to emphasize the interrelationship of each to the other.[10] The interrelationship is signified by the use of the common letter "L." This is consistent with the biblical witness that while the person may be perceived from various points of view, the person is a unity. A practical implication for pastors is that anything that significantly affects a pastor's bodily well-being also affects his or her relationships, and of course the reverse is true. The same thing can be said of each of the other dimensions. Consequently, in our later case presentations, no matter what the starting point or the pastoral problem, we will consider a pastor's whole personhood: body, mind, feelings, and relationships.[11]

Wholeness, of course, means something special to a Christian. Although from a secular perspective wholeness means thinking about persons as physical, mental, emotional, and social beings, the Christian goes beyond this by saying that wholeness also involves a personal center. As a bodily, thinking, feeling, and relating person, we are centered in the values of our faith. For a Christian to be a whole person is to be a believing person, a person *in Christ*.

You may have missed on the (w)holistic model any reference to the spiritual. You also may have noticed that the model concentrates primarily on the *structure* of wholeness. Before showing how the spiritual is represented in the model, we need to see more than structure. We need to know the *dynamic* of wholeness—what energizes and activates the person. Psychology, psychotherapy, and Christian theology each show us a part of that dynamic when they describe the past, present, and future of a person in terms of that individual's history, situations, and choices.

Psychology and Our Life Cycle

Much seminary study proceeds from a historical point of view—the history of the people of God in the Bible, the history of doctrine, the history of the church. Yet there is often very little exposure to the insights of developmental psychology, which is the history of a person.

While the (w)holistic model describes the *structure* of personality, part of the *dynamic* of an individual pastor's personality is based on his or her personal history. In thinking about myself, I know that who I am today as a bodily, thinking, and feeling person is related to who I was yesterday. Personal identity ties my past into the present. This is why some developmental psychologists talk about personality as characteristics that have "continuity over time."[12] In some ways my past and my present are so interwoven that if someone were to ask me who I am, I could honestly say, "I am my history."[13] Of course, then I would have to go on to say what I meant by identifying myself in terms of my past. That is what I intend to do in this section.

I Am My History

The best way to gain an appreciation for the way our personal history is linked to our present identity is through the growing volume of life-cycle literature.[14] Writers in the area of human development sometimes highlight a particular aspect of personhood. Jean Piaget, for example, stresses cognitive development and focuses on our childhood experiences.[15] Lawrence Kohlberg is concerned with moral development, and James Fowler synthesizes Piaget, Erikson, and Kohlberg in his illumination of faith development.[16] Daniel Levinson's primary work was with mature males, and Gail Sheehy generalized and popularized life-cycle research for both sexes.[17] Bernice Neugarten and others focus on the geriatric population.[18]

The person whose work I find most compatible with a (w)holistic approach is Erik Erikson.[19] Erikson is concerned not only about the psychological, but also about the biological, the social, and the cultural facets of human development. Furthermore, Erikson includes value considerations in a way that is attractive to pastors.[20] Because of his effort to embrace so many dimensions of humanness while focusing on how we humans grow to be the way we are, Erikson's theory helps us pastors understand what it means for us to say, "I am my history." He does this in two ways. First, Erikson discusses the entire life cycle, rather than just childhood or maturity. This helps us to review our life as a historical whole. Second, Erikson discusses each of the stages of the life cycle in such a way as to help us see how our history is still alive in our thoughts and feelings and actions today.

A few general observations may help to place Erikson's work in context.[21] Erikson was greatly influenced by the theories of Sigmund Freud, but he believed Freud's view was too narrow and limited. Like Freud, Erikson thinks the early years of a person's life are critical, but he goes beyond Freud by saying those early years need not completely determine the course of later life. Consequently, Erikson is more interested in later life growth and development. Erikson's eight stages cover the entire life cycle, from birth to death. Moreover, Erikson is interested not only in internal development but also in the way the developing person interacts with his or her social environment.

At each stage of life, Erikson believes the person goes through a crisis. There is a specific developmental task to accomplish, and the completion of that task is critical for future healthy development. As we review each of these crucial stages and tasks, we will note some of the ways in which a pastor might still be affected by what went on in his or her life years ago. In many respects, we pastors are our history, but it is important to remember that we are also more than our history.

A Pastor's First Years of Life

Erikson says that our first year of life has great significance for our subsequent development. The key is the kind of relationship that existed between us and our mother (or mother surrogate). Our mother represented the "world." According to Erikson, what goes on between the infant and the mother is that the self finds out how much he or she can trust the world. It is critical for future growth that the infant come out of the first year with more trust in the world than mistrust. Erikson believes the balance of trust and mistrust is never completely resolved on one side or the other. No matter how fortunate the circumstances, no individual emerges from the first year of life with absolute trust. Neither does anyone emerge with total mistrust. It is the favorable balance of trust over mistrust that is crucial.

Most of us pastors were born into a nuclear family, with a mother and father both present during the first year of our life. If not, then there was a parent figure. Our present capacity to approach the world in a trusting way, in Erikson's view, has something to do with the way things went between us and our mother. There can be too much as well as too little mothering, so the situation is more complex than whether or not our needs were met and how we responded. It is probably no overstatement to say that, even today, a pastor bears the marks of his or her earliest experiences. Every pastor has some basic dependency needs. The pastor's confidence in those needs being met or even being of interest to the world (environment, others, the congregation, God) is related to (though not completely determined by) this earliest stage of development.

During the second stage, our critical task was to come out of the second year of our life with more autonomy than shame and self-doubt. We probably do not remember the first time we said no, but it was an enormously important moment. By saying no, we defined ourself as not identical with the mother/world. Significantly, this is also the time when we began to stand on our own two feet. It was the beginning of our sense of autonomy. The dependence of our first year was balanced by the relative independence of our second year.

Around this time, control issues were very important. Our parents and we were very likely locked into a struggle. There was a serious, though probably unarticulated, question of who was in charge. At times we were frustrated by our parents' limit-setting. Although there are dangers when no limits are set, most persons who grow up to be pastors probably had too many rather than too few. If we were overly restricted, we may have heard the message that something was wrong with our impulse toward autonomy. Later in life, some pastors will continue to fight the battle of autonomy and control. Those whose earliest struggle was traumatic and unsatisfactorily resolved may find themselves being more sensitive to authority or other powerful figures and more in need of defending their right to be themselves. In this, as in all other areas of life, our history is always with us.

During the remainder of the preschool years, we had the task of developing our dependence-independence in relation to others by learning to take initiative without feeling guilty. These others were probably our brothers and sisters, if we had siblings, and of course our playmates. When the dependence-independence issues of our first two years of life are not adequately worked through, our movement out into the interpersonal world is a problem. Some pastors are not sure where they stand with significant people in the parish, and they are hesitant to take steps to find out. Others are unwilling to take the risk of initiating a new program or advancing a strongly held personal opinion. Still others are reluctant to assert a personal right. If these are lifelong characteristics, they may be related to how successfully that pastor was able to resolve his or her early developmental crises.

By now, you may be wondering not whether you *are* your history, but if you are *only* your history. The pastor who would be free from his or her history wisely recognizes that freedom is relative. A step in the direction of freedom is to become aware of our personal history and learn from it. We can face the facts of our life with a special courage. The people of God throughout the ages have not forgotten the past. We seek not to deny but to understand our history.[22] The pastor looks to world history as the arena within which God has chosen to work and to come in Jesus Christ. Christ also comes to us in our personal history, however filled with problems. To persons, as to the world, Christ is present not because of the greatness of our story, but because of the greatness of his love.

Life in School and the School of Life

We have stopped the pastor's developmental story at the age of five or six. Freud would have found little reason to go much further. In his view, the personality is pretty much set by this time. Erikson keeps on going and, as a matter of fact, finds in the next stage, which takes in the early school years, some issues very important to pastoral ministry: we were hard at work in school to overcome feelings of inferiority with a growing sense of our being able to do, to perform.

Other psychologists have further emphasized the importance during this period of our life of the development of a sense of competence and mastery.[23] Sociologists have also stressed the significance of the school years for learning to be a productive member of society.[24] If we did not learn the achievement orientation of our society from our parents, then our school experience undoubtedly contributed to our sense that our worth as an individual is related to what we do.

Pastors as persons have to contend with this early and powerful stress on what we later come to know as "works righteousness." Men and women in the seminary often are seen struggling with their history of having been told—by grades or athletic recognition—that their worth is related to their performance. As we shall see later, the seminary may do little to offset this message. Even when we no longer go to school, we continue these lessons of the past when, upon meeting a new pastoral colleague, we identify each other in terms of the location of our respective parishes, the size of our congregation, and the budget (with particular attention to the salary package). Attempting to measure up, which usually has a quantitative base, is a significant source of pastoral stress. Remembering that we are our history may help us see the value of reviewing what we learned about personal worth during childhood. We cannot change the facts of our past, but we can learn from that past so that we do not simply repeat it.

After analyzing the school years, Erikson turns his attention to early adolescence. Perhaps you still remember your feelings during puberty. As at every life-cycle stage, a new relationship with the world was in the making, but the real focus was on ourselves. We were defining and redefining ourselves over against the world. The majority of us acted out this drama in relation, or reaction, to our parents. We shall discuss later how, during times of particular stress in the parish, we may experience some regression to this painful period of self-doubt and identity-diffusion, especially if some of our adolescent identity questions were never fully resolved.

With the emergence of our sexual self, we began to wonder whether or not we would ever be attractive to another person, especially one of the opposite sex. But there were other questions as well. What would we do when we grew up? What and whom would we believe? Our identity is wrapped up in the answers to these questions, and also in our search for the answers. Often in our society, persons, including some who later become pastors, attempt to escape the pain of these identity questions. One of the most common ways adolescents avoid the discomfort of identity diffusion is to "merge" with somebody else. Sometimes this means peer groups in which the teenager is totally absorbed. Sometimes it means ill-advised sexual behavior. While sexual relationships are invaluable in gaining ground on the identity question, if we attempt to find ourselves by premature union with someone else, we most likely postpone the identity crisis rather than resolve it.

True intimacy is possible only when two persons with relatively stable identities freely choose to be together. A couple is not really free if one or both is still fighting old developmental battles. Scars from the past may have been reopened when a relationship is marked by uncomfortable feelings of mistrust, shame and doubt, guilt, inferiority, and/or identity diffusion. Such feelings complicate a person's capacity freely to enter the postadolescent stage which Erikson calls "intimacy versus isolation." Ideally, this is the stage at which young adults further develop the meaning of their personal identity within the context of interpersonal relating. In such close, intimate relationships, there are many risks as well as joys. Some find it difficult to be open, especially when they sense that they are risking and perhaps could lose their hard-won sense of identity and self-esteem. Our early developmental struggles—holding on and letting go—may be reactivated. Sexual relating, at its deepest level, is a crucible for the working through of these issues in one of the most vulnerable areas of life. Sometimes those who become pastors do not really work through this stage, and our risk-taking with a significant other or spouse is limited. As a pastor, we may find counseling in relational situations stressful if the issues come too close to our own unfinished business.

Of course, an individual may choose not to marry. These single persons also must work through the intimacy issues. When we take singleness seriously as a life option, we realize that intimacy and sex are not the same thing. Single persons can have intimacy without sex, just as persons can have sex without intimacy. Such a wider definition of intimacy is valuable when we attempt to provide pastoral care or counseling to a single Christian in our sex-conscious society. Since an increasing number of requests for pastoral counseling include sexual concerns, any unclarified values the pastor has in the area of sexuality will contribute considerably to stress in pastoral ministry. While our sexuality is inseparable from our humanness, our sexual self-understanding is part of our life story. In no other area of pastoral functioning or personal relating is it more clear that we are our history.

The Years of Pastoral Ministry

The last two stages Erikson describes center in the life-cycle tasks that will occupy pastors during most of their personal development throughout their ministry: generativity and integrity. Most of the persons reading this book are now in one of these stages. Erikson identifies our critical task as we move toward middle life as the attainment of a favorable balance of generativity over a sense of stagnation.[25] Generativity means concern for others in a creative and caring way. The birth of our children, and the nurturing of them, as well as a growing appreciation for the needs of others beyond our own household are reflections of the generative concern.

Most pastors can easily identify with the generative task, for our profession is a generative one. Ministry has a strong nurturing component. However, those attracted to the ministry frequently have not only a high need to nurture, but also a high need for nurturance. There are potential problems when the pastor's need *to* nurture is confused with the need *for* nurture.[26] If we have a keen awareness of our personal history, we may better be able to anticipate our problems in this area before they become a problem for someone else.

For Erikson, the fulfillment of development is in the stage of integrity. This is a time when an individual can look back over his or her life cycle and affirm himself or herself, and life. Erikson says that if a person successfully works through the critical stages of life, that person's life is marked by certain virtues such as fidelity, care, wisdom, and hope. Erikson's message is that, even in the face of death, one need not despair when one's life is experienced as an integrated whole. This is the exclamation mark with which Erikson would punctuate the last sentence of life. While we may have difficulty claiming such confidence in and of ourselves, Christians believe that such a yes to our personal story is enabled by God's yes to us in Christ: "For all the promises of God find their Yes in him" (2 Cor. 1:20). Christians agree that the life-cycle task of integrity is fulfilled in true self-acceptance, and we understand our self-acceptance to be grounded in trust and hope of our already having been accepted by God.[27]

In summary, psychology helps us to recognize the importance of our personal history in our understanding of the pastor as a whole person. Our development as a person is ongoing, all the way to our death. Furthermore, the later chapters in the story of our life are continuous in significant ways with the earlier chapters. In this sense our history is always with us. When I say, "I am my history," I need not mean that I am *only* my history. But I do mean to say that my past history is relevant to my personal present. In order not to be unconsciously controlled by that history, a pastor must learn what of the personal past can healthily be integrated into the present, and what needs to be reexamined and reevaluated from the perspective of greater psychological and spiritual maturity. The Bible says: "For freedom Christ has set us free" (Gal. 5:1). As we learn from and integrate our past into our present, we become more free from those early, archaic thoughts and feelings and assumptions that may limit our perspective on life and even our ability to care. As we become more free *from* those limitations, we become more free *for* personal and pastoral response to others.

There are, however, dynamics other than our history that can help the pastor toward greater self-understanding as a person. We learn in seminary to interpret Scripture in its context, and that contextual interpretation is no less critical when applied to the living human document that is our self.[28] The pastor as a person is not only his or her history. Each of us is also intimately interactive with our world, which is primarily a world of others.[29] The segment of the world nearest at hand which engages us most fully is what we call our life situation. There is sometimes such close correspondence between who I am as a person and my life situation that I can appreciate the truth contained in the existential assertion: "I *am* my situations."[30]

The Human System

Tom Daniels and John Jeffrich both wanted to be sure the seminary considered the way life situations affect a person, including the person in ministry. Tom had not mentioned it to the group, but his congregation's building program was beginning to get him down. John's enthusiastic endorsement of a situational approach also came out of his own immediate life situation, a counseling session with Myra Lynn. The issues involved in the Lynns' problems will illustrate what it means for a person—and a pastor—to say, "I am my situations."

Pastor Jeffrich was called by Mrs. Lynn early on the morning of his meeting with Tom, Joan, and Chris. Jennifer, her 16-year-old daughter, had not come home again the previous night. In going to Jennifer's room to see if there were any clues as to where her youngest might be, Mrs. Lynn had come across some paraphernalia which she thought might be related to drugs. Because she sounded so desperate, Pastor Jeffrich set aside his plans to finish his sermon and invited Mrs. Lynn to his study. John asked if Mr. Lynn would also be coming. He was told that Jennifer's father had again gone away on the business that had been taking him out of town these last several months.

Since Pastor Jeffrich had gone to seminary in the 1960s, he had been trained in models of counseling that emphasized pastoral intervention with an individual. In addition, John's father had been a heavy drinker, very probably, he realized later, an alcoholic. A few years ago, John had learned more about alcoholism and the similarities of all varieties of substance abuse. He knew from his childhood the heartache families can experience when someone abuses chemicals. Therefore, by professional training and personal life experience, he felt reasonably confident he would be able to respond to Mrs. Lynn.

Pastor Jeffrich was not, however, fully prepared for everything Mrs. Lynn would tell him. Apparently Mr. Lynn also had a history of drinking, carefully hidden from anyone outside the family. Moreover, he became physically abusive when he was intoxicated and, during the past year, Jennifer had increasingly borne the brunt of his rage. She had begun staying out at night, and Mrs. Lynn suspected she was mixed up with a bad crowd. Right now, Mrs. Lynn was not even sure where she was. John realized that Jennifer probably had many more problems than he had originally thought. He also felt conflict about having to be out of town for the next few days.

For years, John's counseling orientation was to identify a person's problem and then counsel that person up to the limits of his competence. John had learned one-on-one counseling not because it was necessarily the most consistent with the Bible and Christian theology, but because training in pastoral counseling when John went to seminary borrowed heavily from the approach of secular psychotherapy.[31] Initially, the most influential secular approach was that of dynamic psychotherapy, with its Freudian underpinnings. In the dynamic model the emphasis is on what is going on inside the individual. Therefore, the therapist worked intensively with the person being counseled. The dyad of therapist-patient was rarely broken, even to admit a spouse with whom there might be major marital problems. Later, the most influential model was client-centered psychotherapy, utilizing the theories of Carl Rogers. While Rogers' assumptions allowed for more freedom in therapeutic approach, the orientation was still very person-centered. These two perspectives also influenced John's Clinical Pastoral Education, the only training in pastoral care and counseling that Pastor Jeffrich had, other than in seminary. Though there had been some discussion of marital or relational work, and John heard a little about group counseling, for the most part his earlier training in individual counseling had been reinforced.

Fortunately, during his previous pastorate John had attended a seminar on alcoholism. He recognized what had probably been going on in his parents' home and some of the ways it had affected him. He also learned about an approach to counseling called "systems theory."[32] In the systems approach, the "identified patient" would not be determined simply by who used alcohol or by the presence of drug paraphernalia. The problem needed to be evaluated in relation to the Lynn family as a whole. The problem that existed would not be Jennifer, but the family *system*. Along with Jennifer, Mrs. Lynn, Mr. Lynn, even her brother who no longer lived at home, i.e., the whole family system needed to be the focus of Pastor Jeffrich's care and counseling.

One of the primary "teachings" of a systems approach is that, while it is appropriate to consider an individual from the perspective of that person's personal history, it may not be adequate. An equally important perspective is provided by an analysis of the system within which that person lives and functions. In certain respects, systems theory suggests, a person *is* his or her situations.

I Am My Situations

Pastor Jeffrich grew up in a home where there was alcohol abuse. John has a certain history because he learned about life in a special situation. Later in life, John learned that he was not only a victim of that situation; he was also an active participant in it. Jennifer is in a similar position in her family—in some ways a victim and in other ways a participant. In later years, Jennifer's history will include the way her family situation was or was not resolved.

Erikson's developmental scheme, with its psychosocial emphasis, reminds us that the story of a human life is written in relationship to significant others. Whether we accent the pastor's personal identity in terms of history or in terms of life situations is simply a matter of perspective. The pastor as a person learns about himself or herself not only by revisiting the past, but also by reviewing the present situations and relationships he or she is in.

This is consistent with a theological perspective. The Judeo-Christian anthropology referred to earlier is at its heart relational. The person is always a person in relationship. Individual hopes and dreams are always bound with community hopes and dreams. *Shalom* is a right relationship, not only with oneself, but also with one's neighbors.

However, even when we add the social to the physical, mental, and emotional dimensions, we still have discussed only parts of being a person. What integrates the pastor as a whole person—a whole person in Christ? Pastor Joan intuited that it had something to do with personal responsibility and decision making. Perhaps the dilemma she felt herself to be in will help illustrate the way our choices are involved.

Personal Integration

The day had been a long one for Pastor Joan. The lay leader from St. James had telephoned just before lunch, and Joan had been completely unprepared to consider a call to her former internship congregation. St. James was a challenging and vibrant parish in a neighboring state. Joan had not been back in over three years, although she occasionally heard from some of the members. She had learned in one of the letters that her supervising pastor had been appointed to an administrative post a few months ago. Now she had been told that the call committee unanimously wanted to recommend her as St. James' next pastor. Before the committee made their recommendation public, they wanted to know whether or not Joan would consider such a call. Joan asked whether she could think and pray about their inquiry and telephone them around dinner time.

During the rest of the day, Joan had found it hard to keep her mind on her work. Her thoughts kept returning to her internship days at St. James, comparing them with her ministry at First Community Church. First Community had been her first call after seminary, and Joan's election was not accomplished without some controversy. She was the first woman pastor they had ever interviewed. Even though Joan had stressed her commitment to celibacy, some were concerned about the possibility that Joan might meet someone and want to get married. If she did, they wondered what would she do if her husband were transferred or if she became pregnant. Others wondered whether she would be able to handle the pressing problems that had led to the congregation's decline and the previous pastor's resignation. Behind most of the concerns, however, Joan was able to perceive the parish wanting a long, healing pastorate.

Finally, the congregation's misgivings had been overcome and Joan began her ministry. Within two years, the quality of her work had become known even outside her district. That is how she came once again to the attention of the call committee at St. James. The congregation wanted inspired leadership in order to continue St. James' strong program. Many remembered Joan as a most gifted person. In addition to real emotional attachment to some of the people at St. James, Joan also knew that no other female pastor had been given a call to any congregation in St. James' district.

Joan was flattered, but she was also concerned. Over the past year she had been having increasing doubts about parish ministry. No one knew about her disillusionment, but Joan was not at all sure that starting another pastorate was a good thing to do right now. She also wondered what the effects of her leaving First Community would be, especially after the problems the congregation had experienced with the previous pastor. She had grown to love many of the people, and they loved her. But then maybe a new start would change the way she was feeling about herself and her vocation.

As Joan stared out the window of her study, ruminating about the many ramifications, her eye caught the clock on the town hall steeple. She saw that it was almost the time she had agreed to telephone St. James. As she reached for the phone, her heart skipped a beat and she noticed her hand was damp. "Oh, God," she sighed, and the sigh became a prayer.

At this moment, Joan is a vivid example of a pastor as a person. She is reacting to her situation physically, mentally, and emotionally. Furthermore, how Joan's body reacts biochemically, how she cognitively analyzes the problem, and her particular mixture of feelings in circumstances like this are characteristic of Joan. Joan is a person with a particular history, and no other person will bring exactly the same past to the present moment. But Joan is more than her history; she is also identifiable in relation to her immediate situation. The present circumstance is a microcosm, a "little world." This one event gives us an idea of how Joan relates to the world at large, particularly the world of others. As much as Joan can be known through her history, she can also be known through her situation.

How does a pastor with a particular history and a special life situation move toward personal integration? At the pastors' meeting, Joan expressed it exactly. At the heart of the matter is personal choice. Pastor Joan's identity is related to her past history and her present situation, but who Joan *is* will become even clearer to us through the choice she makes.

I Am My Choices

To illustrate the relationship of decision making to the pastor's integrity as a person, we must take another look at the (w)holistic model.

We have already seen that the model represents the self in relation to the world, with the dynamics of a person's past history and present life situation. The interrelationship of all these di-

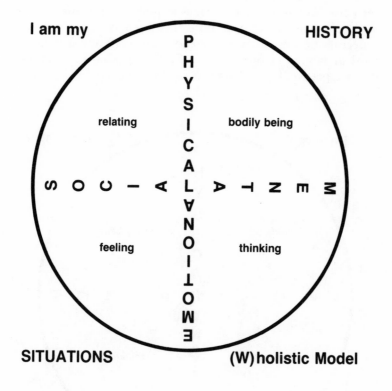

(W)holistic Model

mensions and dynamics is symbolized by the use of a common letter L. However, the interrelating L is used in more than an interactive way. The central L also serves as a mnemonic device, since *El* is a Hebrew name for God. You may have noticed the absence of a "spiritual" dimension on the model. This is intentional. The spiritual is not represented as one dimension among others, but as the integration of each and all of the dimensions, symbolized by the center "L." It is my conviction that there is a God-question implicit in every experience of the pastor as a bodily, thinking, and feeling person, and a God-question implicit in every interpersonal encounter.[33]

Consequently, Pastor Joan's dilemma can be appropriately

analyzed in relation to her physical, psychological, and behavioral response. But an *adequate* analysis requires paying attention to her decision as a theological problem as well. A person's choices reflect his or her values. If the choice is significant, it is all the more apparent that our choices reflect our *ultimate* values. From this perspective, Pastor Joan can say: "I *am* my choices."[34]

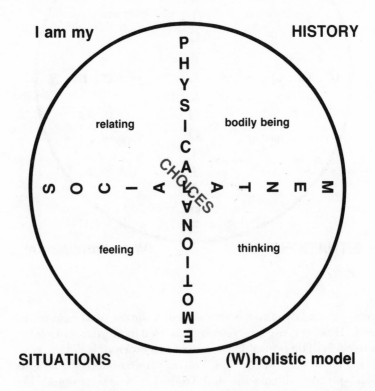

The Bible helps us to understand how central choice is to our personal identity. Moses apprehended this existential reality when he offered in God's name the covenantal invitation: "See, I have set before you this day life and good, death and evil. . . therefore choose life" (Deut. 30:15,19). In the gospel the call to choose life is paradoxically a call to die daily to sin in order that we may be raised to newness of life. In choosing to die to self, we participate in the cruciform character of Christian life.[35] Such choices require courage, and our en-couragement is in Christ's promised presence in the midst of life's anxieties and life's tasks. "I will not leave you desolate; I will come to you" (John 14:18); "Lo, I am with you always, to the close of the age" (Matt. 28:20). With the grace-full promise of presence, every choice is a challenge and no problem situation is without possibility. "I can do all things in him who strengthens me" (Phil. 4:13). These themes of choice, challenge, and Christ provide a biblical framework for a day-to-day living out of a practical Christ-centered ethic.[36]

If, then, we are our choices, how Pastor Joan chooses to handle her stressful situation is central both to her pastoral identity and to her personal identity in Christ. Christian anthropology helps us to appreciate the significance of a person's history, his or her story. That anthropology also requires us to reflect on the relevance of an individual's life situation. Above all, a biblical anthropology alerts us to the integrative nature of a person's choices in the midst of life's challenges.

Our (w)holistic model has been presented in some detail. The assumptions that underlie the model will help us in our analysis of some of the common problems of the pastor as a person. We shall return to Joan shortly, as the significance of her choice becomes even greater when more of her story is known. However, first we need to return to Tom Daniels. We left him after the pastors' meeting, as he was on the way to see his physician.

The Pastor
as a Physical Person

Pastor Tom and Hezekiah's Tunnel

The last time Tom had felt so trapped was when he was in Hezekiah's tunnel. Tom had been on his first trip to the Holy Land with a group, mostly clergy. One day, he was standing near the top of the Mount of Olives, looking across the Kidron Valley to the Golden Gate of Jerusalem. The guide pointed south and said that hidden in one of the recesses of the valley was the cavelike entrance to Hezekiah's tunnel. The long, winding tunnel was carved out by hand through earth and rock about 3000 years ago (2 Kings 20:20; 2 Chron. 32:30). The tunnel is an aqueduct that provided the ancient city a protected source of water. Tom was interested to learn that the water flows out of the tunnel into the pool of Siloam, where Jesus sent a blind man to wash his eyes and be healed (John 9:7). In earlier times King David had led his soldiers up a previous shaft to capture the city of Jerusalem (2 Sam. 5:8). When someone in the clergy group suggested a late afternoon adventure "in the footsteps of David," Tom readily agreed.

The water was colder than Tom had imagined, but what he was not prepared for was the darkness of the tunnel. Only a few halting steps from the entranceway, the brilliant sun was completely absorbed! For an instant, Tom felt alarm and thought of turning back. But one or two of the others in the group had brought flashlights. Their lights, for a few minutes, illuminated the interior. However, since the group had to go single file and those with lights were ahead of Tom, the leaders were able to snake through the long tunnel with relative ease. But with the light dimming, Tom had to walk slower and slower. The sharp stones on the bottom of the stream bed, which he could now feel but not see, slowed him further. As the voices of his small group became more distant, he wanted to call out, but he kept his feelings in. Tom began to feel very much alone.

In order to avoid bumping into the crudely hewn walls and ceiling in the inky blackness, Tom needed to hold one hand out to his side and the other hand just above his head. At points the stream bottom sloped downward and the water appeared to be rising. When this occurred simultaneously with the walls closing in and the ceiling becoming lower, the claustrophobic sensation Tom experienced was overpowering. He wondered if he would drown!

Tom's time in Hezekiah's tunnel was one of the most stressful he had ever experienced. His response was a total reaction. Physically, his nervous system was prepared for fight or flight. There was, of course, no one to fight and no way to run. His heart pounded anyway. His mind reminded him that it was Hezekiah's tunnel, but his rapid pulse beat out "Tom's tomb, Tom's tomb!" He knew he was not the only one in the tunnel, but he felt alone. And he was angry as well as scared. Angry at himself for having gotten into the predicament. Angry that no one had cautioned him to take a light. Angry at those who had lights and had left him behind in the darkness. Though he had entered the tunnel with a group, he had little thought for the well-being of anyone else. His world had collapsed into a black tunnel, squeezing out the world of others. There was only God to talk to, and God had allowed this to happen. There seemed to be no hope.

Nonetheless and unexpectedly, hope revived. Hope took the form of a little Palestinian child. Contrary to the rules governing the tunnel, the little boy had slipped past the guards at the western end of the tunnel, the end toward which Tom would have been heading had he not been paralyzed with fear. The mere presence of the child told Tom there was a way. Tom followed the child to the end of the tunnel, where the water turned into the pool of Siloam. So relieved to be out of the tunnel, Tom lay down by the gathering pool until, like the man in the Bible story, he could get up and return to where he was staying in Jerusalem.

From that time on, when Tom was in a really tight spot, he thought about Hezekiah's tunnel.[37] It was one of those times. Last week ground had finally been broken after a two-year building program that had run into one problem after another. Yesterday, the contractor had discovered quicksand, and the cost factor escalated, to say nothing of the delays. Today, Tom's conference with his physician had been the final straw. How would he ever be able so drastically to cut his work schedule? The doctor simply did not understand! "If anything," Tom thought to himself, "I need to do more. Why did this have to happen now?"

Tom's physician had told him that he simply must get away from work for a while. If that was impossible, he should work no more than half-time for several weeks, then return slowly, but never at the pace he had been going. The symptoms he was having could be caused by overextension and anxiety, but they might also mean Tom was not getting enough blood to his heart. The doctor had discussed additional tests and the possibility of surgery if the tests were positive. The tranquilizers Tom had started taking last year during the fund-raising had seemed to help, but they had dealt with symptoms, not causes. Additional medication now, the doctor advised, would only cover up the symptoms, and that could be dangerous. "In any event," the physician said, "your body is giving you a strong message. You take care of others. You're going to have to take better care of yourself. Even if the tests turn out OK, something has to change!" As those words penetrated his mind, Tom began to feel closed in. His breath seemed to leave him, and he felt very heavy and very old.

Tom was 48. He had finally returned to the physician when the chest discomfort would not go away. He was also feeling a tingling in his left arm that sometimes turned into an ache. Tom's father had suffered from angina when Tom was a teenager. His dad died at 52. Tom did not think of that often, but he did today. The physician took a longer than usual time with Tom, but the waiting room was crowded, and the doctor had to move on to another patient. Tom had not understood everything that the physician said, but he did have another appointment tomorrow afternoon, and he was to bring Jan, his wife. Tom wondered how he would tell her.

Jan was having problems of her own. Unlike Tom, whose parents had both died, she was the only daughter of aging parents. Her mother had recently come home after being hospitalized, and her father was having great difficulty handling her. Jan knew her parents would never ask, but she wondered if she should fly to her parents' home and help. Last week Jan had said something to Tom, who thought it would be all right if she were not gone too long. Jan said she would ask about the possibility of getting released time at her job. Tom knew that Jan would be even more torn now. Tom also feared Jan's resentment, because she had been telling him that he was killing himself, but he would not listen. She no longer wanted to hear about his symptoms.

Tom also wondered what would happen in the parish. The people depended on him. He had been at Messiah for almost five years. It had been an uphill struggle. The congregation had been having trouble attracting younger families after a previous pastorate that had been too long. There was a faithful core, but most of them were tired and ready, when Tom arrived, to pass the leadership on to others or to the new pastor. There were few takers. Tom felt the laity wanted a strong, pastoral presence. Tom had been suggested by the bishop because he was a vital, outgoing man with many ideas and energy to match. Tom had done a good job in his previous parish, but he had been there eight years. When he became 40, Tom began to think of another call. Even though Tom did not feel as young as he once was, he felt quite ready for Messiah.

Anyone who saw Tom at work thought they were seeing a much younger man. What Tom realized, and others did not, was that he had to work longer than he once did to get the same amount accomplished. Over the five years at Messiah, his work week frequently was 60 hours, and during the past year it had been averaging even more. Tom honestly believed that the things that needed to be done required that time commitment.

Jan was not so sure. She, of course, was the one other person who had some idea of the cost of Messiah's success. Jan knew that

Tom was dedicated to his work. She also knew how important it was to Tom that he be loved and respected. She had been concerned for some time that Tom was pushing too hard in order to gain the affirmation he needed. Tom had gone to two services on Sunday with never a mention of needing some assistance. He had started groups for just about every special interest she could imagine. Worst of all, he did not know when to stop. Last summer, Tom had a month's vacation coming. He took a little over a week, because he felt he just could not get away during the building drive. Now, with construction under way, Tom was busier than ever. The harder he worked, the fewer alternatives he saw.

Jan once suggested he talk to someone. She knew Tom was used to doing things on his own, but maybe another pastor could understand and give him some suggestions. Tom had some clergy acquaintances, but no one he felt could really understand. Chris Campbell had an active parish, but he also had an assistant, which made the situation entirely different. Tom had always felt competitive with John Jeffrich, and Joan Russell, like Chris's assistant, was too new and too young. Tom chose to keep his problems to himself.

Jan saw Tom become more and more preoccupied and unavailable even to her. He seemed to get irritated more easily, too. She was tired of hearing him talk about not feeling well when she could see that anyone who worked like that would not feel well. But Jan really became concerned when the chest pain started last month. Tom had tried to minimize it, but she knew it was a different kind of pain from the tension he occasionally felt in his shoulder and chest. She had been pushing him to see a physician. This afternoon Tom finally went. As Jan looked out the window, she saw Tom coming up the walk. He looked wrung out. The first thing he said as he met her at the door was: "It's another Hezekiah's tunnel."

Stress as a (W)holistic Reaction

Recent research has shown that the average pastor is stressed to the point that he or she has at least a 50% chance of a health change as a result.[38] During the early years of ministry or, as in

Tom's case, after a change in pastorates, the possibility of having a stress-related health problem is even higher.[39]

Because the problem is so prevalent, pastors need to know all that they can about stress. Over the years, I have had an opportunity to consider medical, psychological, socio-cultural, and theological perspectives on stress.[40] Later we shall develop a more complete understanding of the nature of stress, but I believe a good beginning is to consider stress as a (w)holistic reaction of a person to frustration, conflict, and/or pressure.[41] In the next section we shall focus on stress as the pastor's *(w)holistic* reaction. For the moment, however, let us simply consider the nature of the reaction itself.

Stress as a Reaction to Frustration

Tom linked the stress he felt after consulting with his physician to the stress he had experienced in Hezekiah's tunnel. Both the tunnel and his parish situation were filled with frustration, conflict, and pressure. Persons feel frustrated when they are confronted by obstacles. The absence of light in the tunnel made it virtually impossible for Tom to master his environment. Similarly, Tom simply could not "see" how it would be possible for him to maintain his ministry on a drastically reduced work schedule.

Another pastor might have felt less or more stress in these situations. How much stress a person feels is related to how he or she perceives the problem. What Tom felt in the doctor's office and on his way home was affected by his age, what was going on at that time in the congregation, how supportive he thought Jan would be, and how closely his identity was wrapped up in his work. Tom's loss of his ability to go about his ministry in his usual way was just one of the many losses that tend to accompany any mid-life transition. At another time in his life, Tom may have been more able to perceive the need for change as not only a threat, but also an opportunity.

The major frustrations in ministry may be related to two fundamental facts of life: time and space. Stress is produced when a person feels there is never enough time. People also experience stress when there appears to be either a too restrictive environment in which to function freely, or a too open–ended environment to manage effectively.[42] Tom experienced both time and space as stressful. He had failed to put livable boundaries around his work, and now he was feeling closed in by the physician's pronouncement. Since many pastors never feel everything they need to do is done, the loss of three or four hours a week can be frustrating. Tom was facing the loss of three or four hours a day.

Stress as a Reaction to Conflict

Tom was not only frustrated by the turn of events; he was also in conflict, which is another component of pastoral stress. We are in conflict when a choice is necessary between two needs or goals. In Hezekiah's tunnel there was a point, shortly after entering the tunnel, when Tom knew that not having a light was going to be a problem. He was in conflict about going on or turning back. He did not want to lose face with his group, so he kept on going. Now, with the physician's diagnosis, Tom was again feeling the stress of choosing between two alternatives, neither of which seemed desirable. If he continued pressing, he might lose his health. If he dramatically cut back, how could he be the pastor he wanted to be? He also wondered if his parishioners would accept less.

One common source of stress is the desire of most pastors to please and be accepted by others. Tom's need to please others led him to care for them in a way that left little time for him to take care of himself—or those close to him. Earlier in his ministry, Tom had struggled to keep some balance between the congregation's demands and Jan's continuing requests for more family time.

Most pastors can identify with Tom's conflicts surrounding his desire to serve selflessly and sacrificially while still being mindful of family needs. In Tom's case, this conflict had long ago been resolved in favor of the parish. Consequently, Tom was not certain how sympathetic Jan would be.

Stress as a Reaction to Pressure

Along with frustration and conflict, a third source of pastoral stress is pressure. Pressure is stressful when we have to go about our affairs faster or harder. In Hezekiah's tunnel, Tom was under stressful pressure to keep up with the group. His safety, he felt, depended on that. This pressure was all the more intense because

Tom was frustrated by the darkness and the sharp rocks in the stream bed. In the parish, Tom had felt stress producing pressure because of what he perceived to be the expectations of his district and his lay leaders. He had done his best to do whatever it took to do the job. Now, with the building program, Tom felt the press of having an even more demanding task and the frustration of having even less time in which to accomplish it. Tom's stress may then be understood as his reaction to his life situation. The pressure Tom felt in the parish led to frustration, and his frustration led to more pressure. Throughout it all, he felt in conflict.

If stress is a reaction to frustration, conflict, or pressure, it could be helpful for a pastor to consider what it is that unites and underlies stressful reactions. The work of Thomas Holmes and Richard Rahe, authors of the best-known stress scale, give pastors a clue to that underlying theme.[43] Holmes and Rahe list 43 life events, each of which has been found to be stressful.

Events	Scale of Impact
Death of a spouse	100
Divorce	73
Marital separation	65
Jail term	63
Death of close family member	63
Personal injury or illness	53
Marriage	50
Fired at work	47
Marital reconciliation	45
Retirement	45
Change in health of a family member	44
Pregnancy	40
Sex difficulties	39
Gain of new family member	39
Business readjustment	39
Change in financial state	38
Death of close friend	37
Change to different line of work	36
Change in number of arguments with spouse	35
Mortgage over $10,000	31
Foreclosure of mortgage or loan	30
Change in responsibilities at work	29
Son or daughter leaving home	29

Trouble with in-laws	29
Outstanding personal achievement	28
Wife begins or stops work	26
Begin or end school	26
Change in living conditions	25
Revision of personal habits	24
Trouble with boss	23
Change in work hours or conditions	20
Change in residence	20
Change in schools	20
Change in recreation	19
Change in church activities	19
Change in social activities	18
Mortgage or loan less than $10,000	17
Change in sleeping habits	15
Change in number of family get-togethers	15
Change in eating habits	15
Vacation	13
Christmas	12
Minor violations of the law	11

Any of these life events could easily produce in most persons some level of frustration or conflict or pressure. But what is there common to all these events that might produce such reactions? A careful look at the scale shows that each of the life events requires a *change*. It does not matter whether the change is generally considered positive or negative. Change always involves physical and psychological stress.

Stress as a Reaction to Loss

Change is stressful because it always involves a loss.[44] In Hezekiah's tunnel, Tom experienced a stressful change in the loss of light. He also experienced a change in the loss of his feelings of self-sufficiency and of his competence to master the situation. These feelings of inadequacy hounded Tom in the parish, where it always seemed as if he could not quite see the light at the end of the tunnel; a little more than he had to offer was always needed.

Tom's frustration, conflict, and pressure were fueled by his fear of loss in relation to his way of doing ministry. Doing, for Tom, was integral to his sense of who he was as a person. His identity was wrapped up with what he did. If he refused to face the loss of his way of doing ministry, he was confronted with the possible loss of his health and life.

Stress is a reaction to loss. The loss may be actual or anticipated. When a loss is perceived as significant, the pastor experiences a crisis.[45] Tom's physical symptoms threatened a change and loss that was very significant for him because his basic sense of selfhood seemed to be at stake.

Whether or not another pastor would have experienced a crisis in this situation depends on several factors. The personality of the pastor is important; some persons accept change much more easily than others. In addition to personality, the nature of the "stressor" is a factor. The stressor is the change event, what it is that is changing or might change. Finally, the pastor's personal and professional life situations are critical elements.

In summary, stress is a pastor's reaction to frustration, conflict, or pressure, at the heart of which lies the threat of life change and actual or anticipated loss. A time of great stress is a critical time for pastors because it confronts us with the question of our identity and what we have become. In other words, significant stress precipitates in the pastor a crisis in identity.[46] How a particular pastor reacts to a stress-related crisis depends on an interaction of the person, the particular type of stressor, and the pastor's situation.

The Pastor as Reactor

The pastor is an *embodied* person. Tom forgot this, and his body gave him signals of distress. He ignored them as long as he could, but there came a time when his body would no longer be denied.

Tom is like many pastors. In a research project on "The Person in Ministry," seminarians and pastors ranked the physical as the least important of the dimensions of the (W)holistic model.[47] The same study revealed both the presence of considerable stress and of physical symptoms usually associated with stress, such as headaches and awakening from sleep not feeling refreshed. Nutrition, physical exercise, and other forms of self-care were at lower levels than for the general population.

These findings suggest that many pastors, like Tom, would not hesitate to tell a parishioner to take care of herself and might even go to extraordinary lengths to see that she received adequate medical services. The same pastor might also preach from the pulpit that the body is the temple of the Holy Spirit. But when it comes to himself or herself, the pastor tends to forget that he or she is an embodied person.

Stress as a Bodily Reaction

Even though we neglect, ignore, or deny it, any change affects our bodily well-being.[48] When the physician told Tom what he thought was wrong, Tom felt as if a weight were bearing down on his shoulders. We are our bodies, and whatever affects a pastor is experienced bodily.

While all stress affects the pastor's body, all stress is not necessarily bad for us.[49] A moderate degree of stress leads to greater mental alertness and emotional sensitivity. Stress prepares our body to meet a challenge. Sometimes meeting the challenge means facing it head-on. Sometimes it means getting away from a threatening situation. We use more complex methods, but we share with all creatures an initial fight-or-flight reaction.[50] Without experiencing some stress, a pastor could not survive as a person. The only way to avoid all stress is to die.[51]

However, when a pastor goes through a significant change, or endures the stress of many changes over an extended period of time, stress may lead to special problems. Tom seemed to be suffering both severe and protracted stress, which finally caught up with him. Tom probably did not realize that he was in such big trouble. After the initial reaction to a stressful parish environment, the pastor often experiences an upsurge in energy and an increase in his or her ability to respond to the needs. In effect, our bodies are giving us everything possible to deal with the stress so as to be able to return to a normal level. Sometimes this power surge is all that it takes. With our adrenalin pumping and our mental wheels churning, we figure out a way to cope. At other times we do not. The adrenalin pumps, but the wheels spin. This is what happened to Tom in Hezekiah's tunnel, where there was no one to fight and no way to run. In the parish, Tom could not figure out how to get off the treadmill and still do the job. How long a pastor can keep that up depends on a variety of factors, including the pastor's age, general state of physical and mental health, a support system, and his or her values. How long a pastor "should" function at such a pace is a spiritual question to which we shall turn later. But one thing is certain. No pastor can function at top speed forever. As a physical person, the pastor has a limit. When that limit is exceeded, and especially if that limit is exceeded regularly, there are predictable physical consequences. The weakest link in our body system starts to show strain. In time, there may be irreversible physical changes leading to death.[52]

Tom's physician wisely confronted him with the need to minister to himself. Medication has its place, and Tom had the benefit of its appropriate use. But at some point it is no longer healthy to silence symptoms. Tom's body demanded a clear hearing. Tom had forgotten that his body is a gift, but how long the lifetime guarantee lasts depends in part on the care the gift is given. When a pastor drags himself or herself out of bed in the morning and presses the day long, only to return in the evening worrying about what is coming up tomorrow, that pastor is not likely to rejoice in the gift of his or her body. There may even be times when this pastor wishes he or she were not hampered by a body that is exhausted before the mind says it is time to quit. But such wishes lead us away from our personhood, not into it.

Stress as a Mental Reaction

Of course, the body is not the whole of the person. Tom's situation has already helped us realize that the body and the mind interact. Physical stress leads to sharper thinking—for a time. But the mind follows the same general pattern as the body: first, alert and keen, then resourceful, then the beginning of disorganization.[53] One of the steps along the way to deterioration is a change in the way we see; the world seems to close in. When Tom was in Jerusalem his world was reduced to a tunnel. Under conditions of severe stress, especially if it is prolonged, every pastor experiences "tunnel vision." Reducing the world to a more manageable size is a way to make the world a little safer. But there is a cost to pay. Keeping those boundaries close means rigidity. The pastor becomes less flexible. He or she is more likely to resort to old, more secure ways of doing things. He or she is less willing to reevaluate and consider the alternatives. The pastor loses a sense of the possible.

You may have recognized many of the characteristics just described as symptoms of pastoral burnout. Because this new way of seeing things happens over a period of time, a pastor may be in the process of burnout without realizing it. He or she may feel as alert and competent as ever, but efficiency and effectiveness is decreasing. In time, he or she feels that something is slipping. In our culture, greater quantity is an understandable way for a pastor to try to compensate for lower quality. Overextension, however, is seldom a lasting solution. In fact, it generally leads to even more restricted patterns of thinking. Tom was heading in this direction, but his body rather than his mind gave him a sharp signal.

Stress as an Emotional Reaction

Along with the physical and mental changes, stress precipitates an emotional reaction. We have seen how stress is linked with change and loss. Therefore, it should not be surprising that one of the emotional reaction patterns to stress is what pastors familiarly see in grief situations. When a pastor is experiencing a stress-related crisis, which in some way threatens his or her sense of who he or she is, the pastor may feel shock, denial, anger, and even despair.[54] Tom was in touch with two of the most common feeling reactions to stress, even prior to his visit to his physician: he had become more irritable and had early signs of depression. Irritability to the point of anger often results from feelings of frustration. Anger that is turned in on oneself is one cause of depression.

While Tom felt the more common emotional symptoms, stress can produce other feeling reactions as well. A less easily recognizable sign of stress is the pastor's failure to react much at all.[55] Emotional underreactivity may be perceived by parishioners as pastoral insensitivity. When a pastor shows some irritability under pressure, most parishioners can relate the reaction to the stressful situation. On the other hand, when the pastor appears not really to care, most parishioners do not see this as a symptom of stress. Probably the pastor does not make the connection either. However, when a pastor feels little emotional reaction to situations that once would have moved him deeply, prolonged stress may have taken its toll. Underreacting may be an unconscious protection against more than what the pastor feels able to handle.

Stress as a Social Reaction

A bodily, thinking, and feeling person expresses him or herself in the world of others. Stress, therefore, is also a social reaction.[56] Tom's peculiar pain in Hezekiah's tunnel was feeling so alone while being aware that others were geographically not far away.

Stress may almost be defined in terms of moving toward or away from people. In the early stages of stress, pastors are more likely to try to make human contact with others to offset the pain of feeling alone. Pride can keep the pastor from calling out or reaching out, as it did Tom in the tunnel, but other factors can also block the pastor. At Messiah Tom had no colleague or consultant available with whom he felt able to discuss his fears of failure. The stress of going it alone is one of the most severe for many pastors, even more so for those in isolated settings. Whatever the setting, however, when the stress is severe enough and long enough, even the desire to reach out is lost. Of course, before that happens, the body can cry out in pain. Our body, then, can be a real friend, however disturbing the symptom. The cry of distress can be a call to change. That is what Tom's body was telling him. Although the symptom first appeared as a physical problem, Tom was totally involved as a whole person. Another pastor may not have first felt the mounting stress physically, as Tom did. However, whether or not stress is initially experienced as a bodily reaction, eventually the pastor's body will be involved if the stress persists.

While any pastor dealing with frustrations, conflicts, and pressures will experience some degree of stress, the *way* the stress is felt and *how much* stress is felt depends on a combination of factors. The main determinants we have identified are the personal history of the pastor, the nature of the stress and the pastor's life situation.[57] In the (w)holistic model, these dynamics are what is meant by saying we are our history, and we are our situations. Applying the (w)holistic model will help us better appreciate the importance of each of these factors and how they relate not only to pastoral stress but also to the pastor's personal identity.

The Pastor's History and Stress

The case study does not provide much of Tom's life story prior to his pastorate at Messiah. When Erikson's work is applied to pastoral stress, it becomes even more clear that a pastor's stress is an identity issue. How a pastor responds to stress says a great deal about who that pastor is as a person.

Erikson properly emphasizes the physical/biological. Heredity is important. Tom is who he is in part because his parents were who they were. In this sense, when I say, "I am my history," that history is larger than my life.[58] In Tom's case, it is significant that his father suffered from angina and died at a relatively young age. A tendency toward physical symptoms of anxiety and some heart problems can run in a family. The way stress is experienced physically may be as much related to a pastor's history as to the stressful situation. It is therefore valuable for a pastor not only to provide a complete physical history to his or her physician, but also for that pastor to ask the physician how the knowledge of personal medical history can be used for preventative health care.

Our history, of course, is more than the history of our body. The primary thrust of Erikson's work is psychosocial. Tom's inability to trust his concerns to a colleague, his dependence on affirmation from others before he could feel good about himself, and his close connection between his work and his personal identity could have arisen in many ways, but they also could reflect things he learned while growing up.

Because each person has a somewhat different developmental history, there may be great variability in stress tolerance even among brothers and sisters who share a similar biological heredity. If a pastor experienced a serious injury or illness earlier in life, that trauma may later affect his or her vulnerability to stress.

Moreover, no two pastors are faced with exactly the same situation. Even if they were, the personal history each of them brings to that situation would result in their perceiving the problem differently. How we react depends on what we perceive. If a pastor perceives a situation as threatening and evaluates it as more than he can handle, the pastor feels stress. That is why Tom was so stressed in the tunnel, and why he was so stressed in learning he could not go about his ministry in the usual way. In both circumstances, Tom perceived that his life situation was beyond his control.

How any pastor looks at things is a complex combination of unique personal history, prevailing cultural conditioning, professional training, and spiritual insight. Perception is perhaps the crucial psychological and theological factor in our consideration of the pastor as a person. Perception largely determines the severity of a stress reaction. An older, experienced pastor may not find very stressful a situation that a younger colleague, facing that situation for the first time, finds extremely threatening. For this reason, some efforts are being made to see whether experienced pastoral colleagues or mentors may be helpful for pastors new to the parish.[59] The concept of mentoring makes good sense from the standpoint of the perceptual factor in stress production and management.

On the other hand, it is not only the young pastor whose stress level is affected by how the situation is perceived. A pastor's life cycle stage may make a difference. Advocating a cause that might result in the pastor being asked to move might be quite threatening to a pastor who had hoped to retire in a particular congregation. A younger pastor may find the situation uncomfortable, but not so complex.

Not all perceptual differences that affect a stress reaction are related to age or experience. A pastor's response to stress may be complicated by the misuse or abuse of alcohol or other drugs.[60] One of the most unfortunate effects of alcohol and other chemicals is the way they affect a pastor's ability to put situations in perspective, which is a problem in perception. We naturally respond to stress as a whole person, but alcohol and other drugs may interfere with this natural capacity, compromising a pastor's ability to make an adequate, integrated response to stress. Ironically, the alcohol or drugs that one may begin to take as stress reducers may well become one of the stress producers, if the use turns into abuse.

Other factors growing out of a personal history affect a pastor's perception and the severity of his or her stress. Pastors who do not feel good about themselves or who are in marginal or difficult socioeconomic situations, may experience more severe stress during a time of change. This happens because both the person and the person's life situation are more vulnerable to disruption.

The Pastor's Situation and Stress

When it comes to stress, the pastoral situation is in some ways similar to that of other persons, and in some respects it is different. In taking a stress measurement such as the Holmes-Rahe scale, pastors would undoubtedly share with others the extreme stress and grief caused by the death of a spouse.[61] But other items on the Homes-Rahe scale, such as divorce, cause stress for pastors in ways that may be quite different from the nonpastor. An adaptation of the Holmes-Rahe stress scale has been proposed for pastors by Roy Oswald of the Alban Institute.[62] Oswald identified the ten areas of stress with the greatest impact on clergy as death of spouse, divorce, marital separation, death of a close family member, personal injury or illness, marriage, serious decline in church attendance, extreme conflict with the congregation, marital reconciliation, and retirement. Allan Reuter notes that with the exception of personal illness, these are all marital, familial, or occupational stresses.[63] Reuter's observation confirms something we have been saying about stress: personal stress is almost always expressed in interpersonal situations.

Another useful study identified the most common stresses for pastors and their spouses.[64] The main stressors, for pastors, included the proliferation of activities, perfectionism, no time for study, role conflicts, "unwelcome surprise," and church conflicts. The remaining stressors included difficulty in organizing, the "goldfish bowl" existence, the need to prove oneself a hard worker, having no pastor-confessor, experiencing unresolved tension from previous failures to master stressors, and being unable to see visible, tangible results of work.[65]

Pastors, like other people, can endure a considerable amount of stress, if it does not last too long. Tom's building program looked like it would be manageable, but multiple false starts and extended delays may sap the energy of the most vigorous pastor whose other pastoral duties continue, whether the building is delayed or not. Unfortunately, stressors may not only be long lasting, they also rarely come one at a time. Multiple stress situations are, by definition, multiple loss situations, and so create considerable anxiety and often some depression. Probably every pastor has had the experience of coming home after an exhausting encounter with an unreceptive church council or contrary church member, only to have the telephone ring, requiring an emergency pastoral visit. When there are multiple stresses over a long period of time, a pastor can lose whatever reserve, or margin, he or she may have had.

Pastoral Isolation and Stress

When persons are in a stressful situation, especially if the stress goes on and on and on, even those who were initially supportive can begin to withdraw and go about their own lives. Over the years, Jan began to accept Tom's preoccupation with the church as his life-style. She may not have been aware of how critical Tom's situation was getting. Pastors in chronic stress situations may find themselves without ongoing support. Every pastor has seen this occur with the bereaved and with those whose chronic health problems confine them to a convalescent or nursing home. But one does not have to be in grief or incapacitated for this to happen. Our society is very achievement- and results-oriented. We want things to happen, and quickly. A pastor in an ongoing stressful situation may find friends getting fewer and fewer. The church hierarchy may seem not to care. Sometimes it seems that even God is not present, and then the pastor really feels alone.

One of the most effective resources in handling stress is a support group to counteract the feeling of loneliness. Yet, when seminarians enter the ministry they often do not find an active support group of colleagues. All too often they experience other pastors as threatened and competitive. Tom felt that he had no colleagues with whom he could talk, although the successful pastors' group meeting might represent a turning point. Sometimes it appears as if no one cares, even though that may not, in fact, be the case. Unhappily, the narrowing of focus that accompanies our reaction to stress (that "tunnel vision") may put a pastor out of touch with potential resource persons.

At times there is a group, but the group never realizes its potential for support because no one is willing to risk being labeled as inadequate or unfaithful. Some pastors feel they are being unfaithful in complaining about stress, and others feel that they are not being faithful unless they *are* stressed. While a pastor's theology may affirm that a person is not God, his or her *practical* theology, as applied to himself or herself, may support a style of service that has no room for human limitations or relaxation. A pastor may be reluctant to identify himself or herself, especially to the church jurisdiction, as any more stressed than any other pastor. He or she may fear some loss of status in the denomination or even consequence to his or her professional future in the church. Female pastors may fear unfavorable comparison with males. Church bodies which have not educated their clergy members to the vocational hazard of stress may unwittingly suggest that the pastor who experiences considerable stress is the exception, rather than the norm.

There is one additional complication in the pastoral situation. Often the pastor's family is involved in the same pattern of life as the pastor, and members of the family may be experiencing similar symptoms of stress. A spouse simply may not be able to offer the support that is needed.

This may have been true of Jan. She not only had a husband with problems; she also had aging parents who needed her. The conflicting responsibilities to each of these persons closest to her placed her under considerable pressure. In other words, not only the pastor but the whole parsonage family may at times be in the "tunnel" and in need of help to get through.

To whom can they turn? It is hard to find persons in the parish with whom the pastor or members of his or her family can really talk, and there are those who question the wisdom of doing so, even if a compatible person can be found. As for the use of professional resources, such as a psychologist or psychiatrist, there are still many pastors who feel there would be a stigma attached to their "going public" with a need to get their life in order.

The pastoral situation contains all the factors that tend to increase rather than reduce the severity of stress. When these factors are accompanied by an individual predisposition to vulnerability to stress, a crisis may be precipitated. How a pastor like Tom copes with a stress-induced crisis may be a pivotal life decision. Indeed, psychologists have observed that the way we cope with stress over time actually shapes the course of our life.[66]

Personal stress, therefore, may well cause a crisis in pastoral ministry. We have seen that the crisis in ministry, for a pastor, is always in some sense an identity crisis, confronting us with both our past and our present. We are our history, and at every significant turning point in life we must come to terms with who we are in the context of who we have been. The call to change is threatening. Can that call also be a challenge?

The Challenge of Stress

The challenge is not how to eliminate all stress from the pastor's life. That is neither possible nor desirable. Nor is it to find the perfect stress-management technique. Rather, the challenge is to let stress teach us something about who we are as persons.

The Bible has helped us to see that we are embodied persons. Stress as a bodily experience is therefore not subject to evaluation as good or bad, right or wrong. Stress is, because we are. But the Bible does not reduce a person to the physical. When the Bible speaks of the body, it is always in relationship with someone or something. The body is but one way to begin to talk about the whole person in relationship with others and with God. Therefore, if we are to learn from stress, we must not reduce stress to a physical symptom. The challenge of pastoral stress is to allow our stress to call us back into unity with ourselves as a whole person, before God.

The Inadequacy of Stress Management

Although healthy and appropriate, stress management misses the mark in three ways.

First, the extolling of the latest and best in stress management is misleading because there is no best. Since we are whole persons, each with a unique personal history and life situation, no one approach to stress management will be effective or even helpful for all pastors.[67]

Second, stress management may miss the mark because familiar techniques can lead us away from rather than toward wholeness. The (w)holistic model can help us identify the primary focus of the most common stress management strategies.[68]

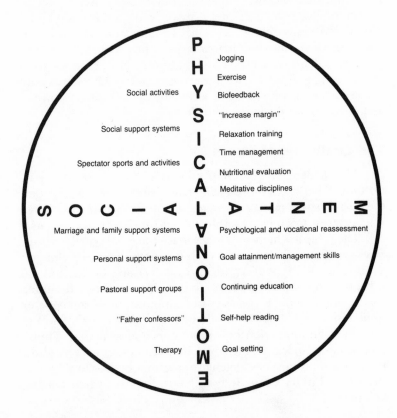

Most approaches to stress management focus on a single dimension of our humanness. Any of these techniques may be appropriate. Which of these resources an individual pastor might find helpful will depend on the personal history of the pastor, the type of stress he or she needs to manage, and the pastor's personal and professional life situation.

If a pastor decides to do something about his or her stress, the chances are that he or she will select one of the forms of stress management listed on the model. There is also a good chance that within six months or less the pastor will fall back into old habits. One study of seminarians showed the "backsliding" rate to be around 70%.[69] For some reason, even an appropriate application of a management technique to the problem of stress appears, in most cases, not to be adequate.

I believe this is because most persons, including pastors, are interested in changing a little, but not enough. Stress management may miss the mark because the challenge of stress is not a call to control a part of our lives, but a call to a much more radical change. Because stress is a (w)holistic reaction, any method of stress management may be appropriate, but an adequate response to stress must attend to all the dimensions of our humanness: physical, mental, emotional, and social, as well as to the "God-question" at the heart of a crisis of stress.

The Challenge to Become Whole in Christ

Pastors' lives can get out of balance, as Tom's did. One symptom of this imbalance is the neglect of one or more of the gifts of our body, mind, feeling, or relationships. The (w)holistic model is particularly helpful in reminding us that any such neglect and imbalance also reflects some loss of spiritual centering. Consequently, however appropriate it is for Tom to *do* something—cut hours or exercise or take a vacation—that kind of change is inadequate. The challenge of stress is to *be* something, to be the whole person we are. Stress has to do with our body, to be sure, but a (w)holistic perspective helps us to understand how any concern of the person is a concern of the *whole* person.

Pastoral stress is the subject of much writing today. Among the most helpful perspectives are those of Lloyd Rediger, Roy Oswald, Charles Rassieur, and Alan Reuter.[70] Rediger and Oswald have written excellent, practical helps for reducing stress and having a more effective ministry. Rassieur's work is quite insightful, quite comprehensive and, like Oswald's, generally compatible with a (w)holistic model. The pastor, however, has to read any such resources carefully. Rassieur suggests an exercise in dis-identification, based on the writing of Roberto Assagioli.[71] The goal of the exercise is to dis-identify with body and feelings in the name of spiritual integration. I think this leads us away from who the Bible says we are. Scripture teaches us how important it is to say: "I am my body, my thoughts, my feelings, my relationships, my history, and my situations." To say that I am more does not require that I dis-identify and thereby disown who and what I am. We are called not *away* from our humanness, but *through* that humanness to God. The incarnation of Christ frees us to be fully human. Only by being who and what I am can I adequately respond as a whole person to the (w)holistic reaction which is stress.

Alan Reuter's approach is not so fully developed as Rassieur's, but his effort to offer a spiritual integration rests on solid theological ground. Reuter says that pastors need to cope with stress through a "paradoxical process of taking charge and letting go."[72] Taking charge involves an active, intentional plan for handling stress. It may include any or many of the techniques listed earlier. On the other hand, Reuter counters the more "works righteousness" orientation of taking charge with the theological necessity of letting go, which involves the acknowledgment of human limitations. "The freedom to let go," Reuter says, "comes in trusting in grace."[73] The paradox of holding on and letting go is resolved when we discern when to act and when to accept our inadequacy and give the problem over to God.

Reuter's notion of paradox is consistent with my research in seminarian and pastoral stress. I have identified a personality type that seems better able than others to handle stressful situations.[74] These theological students and ordained ministers view change not so much as a threat, but as a challenge. They perceive themselves to be choosing persons, rather than persons who are victims of their circumstances. They also experience the presence of a caring Christ with them in the midst of adversity. These are persons and pastors who may be most likely to take charge, when that is appropriate to do. They may also be those who discern that they are not alone, and therefore need not handle the stress as if everything depends on them.

In reading William Hulme's book on pastoral care and counseling, I came across a quote attributed to Søren Kierkegaard.[75] Kierkegaard once said that in order to move *from* the spot, a person must move *at* the spot. Applying that insight to pastoral stress, I would suggest that most of us want to move out of the uncomfortable place in which we find ourselves, without really changing. However, if there is no real change, nothing stays different very long. When we are stressed, we can learn a new technique and use it to get more comfortable, but soon we find ourselves back where we started.

What might moving *at* the spot involve? Real growth in life and in faith comes from accepting responsibility for doing what we can, and accepting our inability to do all that is necessary. We must come to the point of recognizing that even our best efforts to control our lives are ultimately not good enough. Christ alone is the solid rock on which a (w)holistic response to stress can stand. Stress reminds us of our limitations, and our limitations remind us of our mortality. An appropriate and adequate response to pastoral stress must recognize the existential questions that are raised, the human responsibility to use what God has given us, and the theological truth that in and of ourselves we can do nothing. When we have in this way moved *at* the spot we have already begun to move *from* the spot. Then, we are ready to address (w)holistically the problem of pastoral stress—not to save our life, but better to serve with the gift of our life, our body, mind, emotions, relations, and commitments. With this discernment, we lift stress above the level of a problem and allow it to illuminate the truth of our life and the trustworthiness of our God.

The Pastor as a Thinking Person

The Liberation of Pastor Joan

When Joan Russell accepted her first call nearly three years ago, she was determined to be everything anybody could possibly expect of a pastor. Her high ideals and standards were attractive to the lay leadership of First Community Church. The call committee, perhaps because of the circumstances under which the previous pastor had resigned, had very high expectations of an ordained minister. Joan's expectations of herself were even higher. First Community Church had never before had a female pastor, but Joan's friendliness combined with her performance in seminary and her outstanding recommendations overcame any initial reservations. Joan was determined to show the congregation that their confidence was justified.

Joan had always been people oriented. It had been hard for her to leave her old seminary friends behind when she took the call to First Community. The initial excitement of really being a pastor caused Joan not to miss them too much, but soon she began to think about the old crowd. She had become very close with a group at school. At first it was a matter of survival. Being a woman in a predominantly male seminary made her feel uncomfortable at first and unsure of her acceptance. The small group of supportive seminarians had helped her get through those early feelings. Later, when she felt more secure, the group met other needs and she was seldom seen without one or another of "the gang." Saying goodbye had been hard and, of course, they comforted each other that they were not really saying goodbye. Joan had looked forward to making many friends in the parish.

Joan was not quite sure when she realized that having large numbers of people around is not the same thing as having a supportive group of friends. She also began to realize that a pastor-parishioner relationship is not the same as a peer relationship, especially when parishioners expect a special person to be living in the parsonage. But in the beginning, Joan, not conscious of how alone she was feeling, launched into her full-time ministry with all the energy and enthusiasm and excitement she had. Joan had high hopes for the living out of her faith with those she had been called to serve.

During the first six months of her ministry at First Community Church, Pastor Joan seemed to be able to be the minister she had hoped to become. She felt adequately trained to do the work and enjoyed the opportunity, after all those years of preparation, to be doing it. Unlike some of her classmates who had accepted staff-ministry positions, Joan had the relative freedom to develop her own direction in ministry. In particular, she liked to experiment with preaching styles. The warm congregational response helped her to feel liked and respected. Joan sometimes suffered from self-doubt, as she had in the seminary, but she was reasonably confident that she would succeed and she felt personally responsible to do so.

Situations, however, have a way of changing. Some speak of a "honeymoon" period in the ministry. Anyone who knows anything about honeymoons knows that they are pleasant, but not very well grounded in reality. Things simply are not what they seem to be, and the eroding of Joan's perceptions was disheartening to her.

When Joan came to First Community, everyone seemed the same—welcoming, enthusiastic, happy, eager to help. Joan thought, "This is what the communion of saints is all about." Before long, Joan saw that *communion* does not mean *commonality*. The people were really quite different from what they seemed to be at first. Moreover, once Joan began to call on the "inactives," she learned that, far beyond *communion*, even a sense of *community* was missing. The needs of the people and their individual expectations of her were varied and complex.

Joan soon found herself being asked to respond to counseling situations of which she had never dreamed, let alone been prepared. While she knew it was unrealistic to expect that her seminary could anticipate and train her to handle every possible counseling problem, it still came as quite a shock to Joan when she realized she did not have an answer for a particular person or problem. It was much harder than she thought it would be to say, "I don't know." Joan did not want anyone to think she was unequal to the task.

As time went on, Joan found what all pastors eventually discover—that some ministry goals take a long time to reach, if they are attainable at all. Joan had a vision of what a Christian congregation could be—a caring fellowship and a change agent in the community. There was affirmative response to her work to build fellowship in the congregation, but the more prophetic stance in relation to the community required Joan to become actively involved outside the parish and to take some positions not shared by all the members. There were some rumblings, and Joan learned that rarely is change accomplished without someone getting upset. Joan's need to be liked and approved and her need to succeed began to be in conflict with her need to offer a ministry with integrity.

To complicate the matter even more, Joan had to come to terms with the fact that she was inadequately prepared in areas other than counseling. Some of the other tools she needed to accomplish her leadership goals were simply not there. At first, Joan's board members had given her a lot of help in understanding the history of the parish. But then they expected her to pick up the ball. More and more, she began to realize how much of an administrative role the pastor has. Yet, Joan had virtually no training in parish management. Joan's knowledge of how to run a parish was based on her observation of her internship pastor, who had had no formal training either. Consequently, Pastor Joan was not skilled at goal setting or delegation. As the needs and problems at First Community increased, Joan felt all the more responsible and all the more inadequate to handle the situation. She feared the nonapproval that she was certain would accompany any failure.

Another crucial skill Pastor Joan lacked had to do with herself as a person. Joan had not been guided in seminary in how to identify her own thoughts and feelings and how to find appropriate ways to express them. Consequently, she was out of touch with some of her feelings and uncomfortable with those she was beginning to recognize. One of those feelings had to do with her sexuality. Joan was single and had always thought that being single would be an advantage in the parish. She had stressed that point during her pastoral interview. Many times she had discussed celibacy with her seminary group. However, as time went on in the parish, Joan counseled couples planning marriage and parents wanting their children baptized. Before long, Joan began to question whether the single life was really her gift. But the demands of the parish left her with little time for herself. Even when she could break free for a few hours, she felt a conflict between her personal needs and her pastoral role. She wondered how a female pastor goes about meeting eligible young men and what the consequences for her ministry would be if her congregation knew she was "looking."

As neither her professional nor her personal goals were being met, Joan became more frustrated. She was aware of feeling angry. She found it hard to reconcile her angry feelings with hymns like "They'll know we are Christians by our love." More and more, she became uncomfortable with the disparity between what she believed and what she felt. She also wondered how she would be regarded if her parishioners knew what was going on inside her.

By the beginning of her third year, Joan was wondering whether the parish ministry was really for her. It was not that things were going so badly; it was just that the spirit was gone. She was no longer feeling excited, and preaching was getting to be a chore. She was finding it harder to pray, and she had not picked up the Bible, except to prepare a sermon or do some pastoral act, for a long time. Her relationships were deteriorating, too. Her social life was almost nonexistent. Once, the parish activities provided some outlet, but that was changing. Joan no longer looked forward to the monthly board meeting. She even found herself becoming more irritable and impatient with the volunteers who had been so much help at the church office. Most days, she had to push herself to leave the parsonage. After all she had given up and gone through to get into the parish, Joan did not understand why she was so disillusioned and unhappy. She was also aware that she was terribly lonely.

At the three-year point in her ministry, Joan was in crisis. Her ministry hung in the balance. The changes that had occurred since she came to First Community once had seemed challenging, but now they seemed threatening. Earlier in her pastorate, Joan threw herself into her work, confident that she would resolve any problems. During the past year, she seemed to lose the sense that she could overcome the obstacles. She did not see many options in her situation, and she began to wonder where was the God who had promised to be with her always. Her personal and pastoral crisis had become a spiritual crisis. Joan could not shake the idea that problems were a sign of weakness. Only once in her life, at the seminary, had there been a support group with whom she could share her most troubled thoughts or tangled emotions. But she was a student then. As a professional now, even more as a *female* professional in a "male" profession, Joan simply did not feel free to reveal herself as needing help.

The breakthrough came in a strange manner. She received a call to St. James, the church in which she had interned. Joan was pleased about having been asked, but also deeply disturbed. She knew she was not at peace with herself. Another call represented a way out, but she knew it was not the answer. Just as she was about to telephone the St. James committee, there was a knock on her office door. It was Paul Denning, Chris Campbell's assistant at St. Peter's.

Paul had just returned from being out of town. He, like Joan, was fairly new to the community, and the two had not had much contact except at the sunrise service last Easter. Paul looked depressed and asked if he could talk with her a few minutes. Joan was half relieved that she could postpone her telephone call a little longer. Paul wasted no time. It was clear that he needed to get some things off his chest. He told Joan how hard a time he had been having making the adjustment from seminary to his assistant pastorate. He spoke about his frustrations with the senior pastor and, when Joan listened without judgment, he went on to his deeper concern. Paul described some thoughts and feelings he had been having when counseling female parishioners. Nothing had happened yet, but he knew he needed to do something before there was a problem. When he tried to tell his wife Peggy that perhaps parish ministry was a mistake, she had become very anxious about how they would keep their young family together. Paul said that maybe he needed a counselor, but before he took that step he could sure use a friend. He asked Joan if she would be willing to get together a time or two and help him sort out his feelings and frustrations so he could decide what he should do.

Joan's heart leaped within her as she realized what strength there was in Paul's "weakness." She knew that her answer, as well, lay not in running from her questions and her fears, but in facing them. Paul's courage had shown her the way. This was the beginning of the liberation of Pastor Joan.

Tunnels and Transitions

Joan's pastoral ministry was a little like a Hezekiah's tunnel. She entered the ministry conscious of following in the footsteps of those persons of faith down through the ages who have witnessed to God. There were high hopes and expectations, and a great deal of enthusiasm at the beginning. However, it was not long before Joan realized that she could not substitute the warmth of zeal for the needed light. As her vision faded, she began to feel stuck and alone and very unfree, not only as a pastor but also as a person.

As we have seen, not everyone has the same experience in a Hezekiah's tunnel or in the parish. New pastors do not necessarily go through a crisis. However, the first three to five years in ministry do seem to be among the hardest.[76] Even if there is no crisis, the early years in the parish require some adjustment in perception in virtually every pastor. Most weather this period, but if the young pastor does not learn from it, he or she will be less well prepared to handle the critical periods that typically occur around the eighth to tenth year and then again the 20th year of pastoral ministry.[77] Among those who experience real crisis and impending burnout, not all "survive." While the numbers are not overwhelming, the church does lose caring and capable people like Joan.

Pastor Tom gave us the opportunity to consider the pastor as a *physical* person. We shall use the case of Joan to help us understand the pastor as a *thinking* person. Our goal is not to discuss the intelligence of pastors, even though the intellectual level of ordained ministers is generally good.[78] Neither are we primarily interested in what pastors think about the church or the congregation or particular functions of ministry. What we want to pursue is how the pastor thinks of him or herself, both as a pastor who has a certain role, and as a person. Where there is conflict between the person and the role, as there was with Joan, the satisfactory resolution of this conflict is liberating. It leads not only to personal freedom, but also to more faithful pastoral ministry.

How a person thinks says a great deal about that person. "What he thinks is what he really is" (Prov. 23:7 TEV). How a pastor thinks is related to how a pastor perceives. How a pastor perceives is related to the personality of the pastor. Our task then is to consider the person of the pastor, especially the way a pastor's personality affects his or her perception of the pastoral role.

The Pastoral Personality

Joan was quite likable, a "good" person. She tried to do what she thought was right. She enjoyed people and valued warm, friendly contacts. She was generally accepting and trustful. Joan struggled with doubts, as does everyone, but she believed that life has a deep meaning and purpose. Joan wanted to share this faith and hope, because she cared about others.

Having said this, it is important to remember that Joan was just a person. Like everyone else, she was her history. Her personal past was reflected in her personality. Her life story was filled with experiences that contributed to the way she saw life. Joan also had a faith story, which included her sense of having been called to the ordained ministry. That encounter with the Holy Spirit, whether dramatic or a dawning realization, also shapes a pastor's perception. Our life stories and our faith stories interact.[79] It is important for pastors to know what they can about both.

Pastors seeking to learn more about themselves frequently find vocational-assessment and career-development programs useful.[80] Psychological testing can provide a great deal of information in a surprisingly short period of time, and reflection on the findings can be fruitful.[81] Others may find a supportive person or a support group helpful in binding the wounds from the past and recognizing the opportunities in the present. Those who learn from reading might share my enthusiasm for the psychological perspective of David Shapiro, the learning style theory of David Kolb, and the personality theory of Carl G. Jung as elaborated by Katherine C. Briggs and Isabel Briggs Myers.

I have found Shapiro's approach especially helpful for pastoral self-understanding. Shapiro writes about personality styles. He observes that different people have different styles or ways of perceiving, thinking, feeling and behaving. While he says that it is not always easy to identify, Shapiro believes that if you want to understand a person, you must know that person's personality style.[82] Kolb broadens the picture by suggesting that not only individuals, but groups of individuals—like engineers, counselors, or sales personnel—have certain styles.[83] Jung's theory of psychological type is the theoretical basis of the Myers-Briggs Type Indicator (MBTI). The MBTI emphasizes that individual differences are gifts, and the MBTI perspective is of great relevance to ministry.[84] Taken together, Shapiro, Kolb, and the MBTI can be quite instructive for us as we ask ourselves whether there are any identifiable characteristics that generally hold true for those who are interested in the ministry. Is there a "pastoral personality"? I believe the answer is paradoxically no and yes.

First, no. There is no one personality style that characterizes persons either in the seminary or in the parish.[85] God can, and does, call people with quite varied histories and personalities to accomplish the many faceted work of ministry. One need only turn to the gospel accounts to recognize the vast personality differences among the chosen apostles. The gospel stories also show that no person is forever locked into the personality style they have developed. Faith leads to change and growth. "If any one is in Christ, he is a new creation" (2 Cor. 5:17). People at various stages of life and growth are called to God's work.

Common Characteristics of Clergy

But our question about a "pastoral personality" must also be answered with a yes, if we are speaking generally.[86] Persons interested in the ministry typically share certain characteristics, even though they may have very different life stores. You will notice that all of the dimensions of the (w)holistic model are active when we describe what has been called "the helping personality."[87] Most seminarians and pastors are extroverted. They are people oriented and sociable. They are interested in things that directly affect the lives of others. They have strong needs for supportive interpersonal relationships. They are able to work with groups and assume a leadership role. They like to have their work recognized and valued by others.

Most pastors are more at home relating to the outer world of people and events than to the inner world of ideas. They like to look for relationships and possibilities among people and events, although a sizable minority would rather work with facts than possibilities. Their judgments are based more on personal values than on impersonal analysis and logic.

Persons interested in the ministry tend to be idealistic, moral, work-oriented, responsible men and women, who are responsive to the needs of others. They are generally concerned for what others need and want, and try to respect those feelings. Frequently, seminarians and pastors are ambivalent about authority, both being receptive to authority and somewhat resentful of it. Pastors are leaders, but they tend to be quite dependent on what others think, feel, and want. While this contributes to their sensitivity to others, it can also lead to a potential dependence-independence conflict in the pastoral leadership role. Pastoral leadership is also affected by the clergy's tendency to like things orderly and harmonious, and their preference for a planned rather than a spontaneous and more flexible approach to life.[88]

While seminarians and ministers are people oriented, they seem to have difficulty accepting their own humanity. They tend toward perfectionism, with its unrelenting demands on the self. They tend not to take care of themselves physically. The pastor's own thoughts and feelings can be troublesome, particularly if they are not thoughts and feelings the pastor thinks he or she "should" have. Sexual feelings and fantasies can present special problems. Anger, in particular, is problematic for the pastor. There is a tendency to control the expression of feelings, which may account for a typical nonaggressiveness, even passivity among pastors. Their need to control emotion is especially true for negative feelings, which the pastors may believe to be inconsistent with their self-image or unacceptable to others. Image is important, and most pastors are not comfortable with being seen as less than they believe they "should" be.

Pastors seem to need to be in control of their situations, but because the ministry is an open-ended profession, it is difficult for a pastor to feel in control. One way a person can feel more on top of things is to be personally involved in everything that is going on. In the parish this is impossible, and the pastor is vulnerable to the unhealthy consequences of such overcommitment.

You may have recognized that some of the personality characteristics we have identified, such as perfectionism, work orientation, and control, are usually associated more with law than with gospel.[89] These characteristics can also lead to the burnout track Pastor Tom was on and to the kind of crisis in ministry that Joan experienced. As a matter of fact, Joan's approach to her first parish was probably typical for new pastors. Being a woman and single created some additional pressures, but many pastors will be able to see themselves in some of her role conflicts.

When we speak about personality issues, we are always talking about the person as history. Personality development is a process, as Erikson has taught us, that begins early in life and continues throughout life. Any of the typical personality traits that applied to Joan would have some relation to Joan's history as a person. This includes her exposure to religious understandings, especially early in life, during which time she apparently learned that God loves a lot, but he also demands a lot. Joan seems to have felt both the need to measure up and the frustration of never quite making it. How much of this learning came from what her parents said—and did—is unknown, but, for most pastors, the messages in early life from parenting figures are intertwined with later religious beliefs and practices.

We must take Joan's history seriously, but we know that Joan is not only her history. Joan is also her situations. Her immediate situation was the parish itself and the role Joan was called by a

congregation to fill. Was there anything about that role that created a special difficulty for Joan as a person? Another situational
factor which was still alive for Joan was her seminary preparation.
Did the shaping that took place in the seminary help Joan to deal
with herself? Did it help her anticipate the conflicts between her
pastoral role and her personal life, or did her seminary experience contribute to the problem?

Losing Oneself in a Role

The personhood of the pastor is frequently swallowed up in
the pastoral role. Perhaps Joan was even more susceptible because of her feeling that she would be compared to the performance of ordained male ministers, but it is really quite common for
pastors of both sexes to lose themselves in the pastoral role. There
are several reasons for this.

First, the church's expectations of ordained ministers are exceedingly high.[90] A brief review of what was expected of Joan will
illustrate. The pastor is to be a person of faith and integrity,
serving without regard for recognition and providing a responsible, Christian example for all. Her spiritual maturity and discipline were to be exemplary. Joan was "to live and speak so that
the ministering Christ's own caring ministry was reflected in all
that she said and did."[91] In addition, she was expected to represent the congregation not only among the local clergy, but also in
the community and the church at large. She was to reach out
perceptively to others in stressful situations and not to allow her
own stress to interfere with her ability to serve others. In addition,
she was the "resident theologian," responsible not only for teaching but also for modeling the faith.

Many of these expectations are things a person can *do*, and
most of them take a great deal of time to do. The open-endedness
of parish demands and the busyness of the pastor can tempt pastors to continue going through the motions long past the time
when they need to stop and be personally refreshed. In other
words, self-denial, taken to the extreme, leaves little room for
healthy self-care. When this happens not as the exception but as a
way of life, the person is lost in the role. It is likely that a pastor's
spouse or family, if he or she has one, will notice this even before

the pastor, but after a time there will be some symptom of this person-role dis-ease that shows up in the way the pastor physically feels, or thinks, or emotionally feels, or relates.

A second reason for pastors being vulnerable to being lost in a role relates to their training. We might have expected that Joan's ministerial training would have been precisely the place where potential person-role conflicts would be identified and worked through. However, while the seminary is an excellent place for persons to learn about being a pastor, there is much less help in the seminary for coming to terms with the pastor as a person.[92]

A Seminarian Learns the Pastoral Role

Joan came to the seminary straight from college. Since she had not studied Greek at her state university, she began her seminary studies with language so she would be prepared for her biblical studies and be able to translate the lessons for preaching. Her first classes were all required and the courses were academically oriented, with much content to memorize. When the courses had an applied component, the application was almost always how to minister, rather than helping Joan to understand the relationship between the materials of the course and herself as the person who would do the ministering.

Joan's seminary had a contextual program to supplement the academic learning, but even there she quickly fell into a "junior pastor" role. Her supervisor, who had never had any contextual experience during his seminary training, did his best to provide a good role model of an active pastor hard at work. He did not share many of his present personal frustrations and none of his past personal struggles in adapting to the ministerial role. He looked as if he was so "together" that Joan never thought to ask about the personal aspects. Joan's seminary did not require Clinical Pastoral Education, and Joan did not enroll for it. She heard from some other students that CPE was a growing time for them, but she had a full schedule, especially having to fit language into her curriculum.

What Joan did learn, and very well, were the biblical images of ministry, such as priest, prophet, and shepherd. She was especially asked to consider ministry in relation to the image of Christ, who "came not to be served, but to serve, and to give his life as a ransom for many" (Mark 10:45).[93] Jesus' loving self-sacrifice was the highest model for ministry, she learned, and ministry was always to be freely offered without thought of getting anything in return.[94]

Joan also read historical perspectives on ministry and learned that while the pastoral role is always oriented to serving, that service has not always had the same focus.[95] The role of the pastor changes according to the circumstances and needs of those receiving ministry.[96]

Because of the socio-cultural context of the early church, the pastor was called on to sustain and reconcile the people of God. When Christianity became the religion of the Roman Empire, the pastor needed to be more of a guide, especially for converts in need of instruction. Guidance was also needed, and sometimes prophetic leadership, when the church stood against social injustice. At other times, the pastoral role centered more in a priestly ministry of healing—restoring persons to health and wholeness in this life or preparing persons for the next.

Of course, we are only referring to different *emphases* in different periods of history. In responding to the needs of persons, *all* forms of ministry are needed. In addition, healing, reconciling, guiding, and sustaining are not only ways for the pastor to shepherd the Christian community. Ministry is intended to lead to mission. Through ministry the pastor seeks to empower and equip God's people for work in his service, in the church and in the world.[97]

The role of the pastor changes not only at different times, but also in different places. A pastor serving in a European country that has a state church assumes responsibilities that would be unfamiliar and perhaps offensive to clergy in countries where state and church are separate. A pastor ministering to a congregation in a small Alpine or Appalachian village might have a much more central role in the lives of all the villagers than a pastor serving a congregation in a suburb where four or five denominations are represented and the people are highly mobile.

Joan was taught that the history of pastoral care was important for her to know, and she gathered that somehow or other this knowledge was relevant to the shape of the ministry she would undertake. She did not, however, know how to discern the balance of these ministries needed in the parish she was called to serve. She had an excellent theological training, but she was not certain how to apply what she had learned in the concrete and changing congregational context. Consequently, Joan did what most pastors in similar circumstances do: She went about her ministry in the role most familiar to her. That role had much less to do with biblical and historical models than it did with sociocultural and parish expectations. It was a role that reflected her years of growing up in a striving middle-class home and in a parish where her home pastor was a living reflection of America's activistic, achievement-oriented society.[98] Joan had learned that a person is what she or he does, and that personal worth is measured against this standard. College had done nothing but reinforce these attitudes and behaviors.

That performance orientation had not been significantly changed by Joan's seminary experience. On the contrary, just as in college, she had found her theological training to emphasize book learning and cognitive mastery of content. Also as in college, there was a high degree of competitiveness among her peers for top grades and the "best" placements on internship and in the first parish. "Best" might be defined in a number of ways, but it usually had some quantitative base.

The Seminary's "Practical" Theology

While the theology Joan learned in seminary was grounded in grace, the way of going about teaching and learning and living had many of the characteristics of salvation by works. Since this "works righteousness" had been the general emphasis through most of her earlier life, Joan understandably had difficulty internalizing the meaning of grace, even though she received an A in systematic theology.

It was not really surprising, then, that Joan "worked" her way through seminary, just as she had through college. She tried to learn the things that made for success in the parish, because fear of failure had plagued her throughout the years. In ministry-oriented courses, Joan was especially interested in what worked. She did not always stop to consider whether or not what worked was consistent with the biblical anthropology or the systematic theology she had learned. She was better at applying theology to a situation than she was at looking at a situation and thinking theologically about it. Consequently, she was better trained and more inclined to provide answers than she was to listen for the questions people were raising with their lives.

In fact, Joan's role consciousness was so strong that she never seriously questioned whether or not her understanding of the pastoral role left any room for her as a person. That her role models were male and that they may not even have been appropriate models for the fullest expression of her personhood in ministry was never questioned. Joan had demonstrated that she could do what the role "required," and, if there were a cost to herself as a person, she considered it to be the cost of discipleship. No one corrected this misperception.

But this was not the whole story. Somehow, despite the early indoctrination and the lessons over the years, Joan was aware of the inconsistencies in her life and in the church. Joan's personal faith commitment was clear. She longed for a truly grace-full ministry, one that would be more faithful than that which she had received, one that more closely matched what she had been *taught* in seminary, even though she had not observed that kind of ministry in consistent practice. Because of her abiding faith, Joan's crisis in ministry became a turning point. She had lost herself in the pastoral role. Through her conversations with Paul, Joan not only provided a ministry to him. She also began to see herself once again not only as a pastor, but as a person in Christ.

Finding Oneself in Christ

At the heart of the matter of the pastor as a person is the question of personal identity: the pastor as a person, a person in Christ. A recent denominational document on expectations of the ordained states: "First and foremost the church expects its ordained ministers to be believing and practicing Christians, women and men who not only know the Lord but know Christ as their Lord.... The performance of ordained ministry is profoundly linked to ministerial identity. Who an ordained minister is as an ordained minister plays a critical role in shaping what she or he does and how it gets done."[99] This statement comes close to the central theme of this chapter, although I think pastors are helped when a church explicitly acknowledges that *personal* identity precedes even ministerial identity. In addition to linking performance with identity issues, another strength of this document is that the entire discussion of identity is placed in the context of a relationship with Christ.

The problem Joan experienced was that she had good training, but it was *formal* training. That is, she learned the *forms* of ministry without learning the *dynamic* of ministry. The dynamic is supplied by the Spirit-guided interaction of the person of the pastor with the pastoral role. Another way to say this is that the history of the person interacts with the ministry situation. The choices that are involved in the living out of this interaction reflect the person's level of spiritual integration.

Wholeness in the Seminary

The seminary that helps students to become aware of themselves as persons and to comprehend the theological implications of such self-understanding has performed an invaluable service and ministry. The seminary can be a place of great personal and spiritual growth for the seminarian. That growth touches the whole person. Physically, the seminarian can be guided to understand the balance that is needed for a healthy life-style, the nutrition that sustains it, and the exercise that maintains it. Socially, in the comparatively protected environment of a theological school, the seminarian can be relatively free to experiment with new, risky interpersonal behaviors, with the support of faculty and peers. Many persons, pastors included, mistakenly sense that their emotions are beyond their control and tend to blame others for how they feel.[100] Seminarians can learn how to take personal responsibility for their own feelings and learn appropriate ways of expressing them. The seminarian can learn a responsible assertiveness that respects one's own rights and those of others.[101] Values can be clarified and challenged for consistency with biblical truths. Each of these forms of self-care can lead to the seminarian's bringing to parish ministry a more integrated sense of self, and demonstrate the truth that "who a minister is determines what she or he does and how it is done."

In this chapter, however, our focus is on the pastor as a *thinking* person. We have already noted the link between thinking and perception. The seminary is one of the most appropriate settings for perceiving that persons' attitudes and feelings and behavior are related to the basic assumptions these persons make about life. Discerning these assumptions can go a long way in a pastor's attempt to understand the people he or she serves. Of course, pastors are hardly prepared to make these discernments in the parish if they have never been helped to make an open and honest *self*-inquiry. What is needed is training in perception, which some have seen to be the most important education a seminarian receives. John Benton Jr. concluded after an extensive study of Episcopal pastors that "Whether a [person] is an effective pastor seems to be far more dependent upon how [the person] perceives than what [he or she] specifically knows or does."[102]

Pastoral Perception

Benton's research was sponsored by an Episcopal diocese. He attempted to determine whether two groups of pastors, one designated "effective" and the other "ineffective," could be distinguished by how they looked at people and problems. Benton found that pastors who perceived themselves to be just people, like everyone else, are more effective than those "who perceive themselves to be isolated, or insulated, from the rest of humanity."[103] The difficulties some pastors have in accepting their humanity, sometimes expressed in perfectionism and usually involving nonacceptance of negative feelings, stands between the pastor and those he serves. But if pastors are to offer a grace-full ministry to others, they need to experience personal acceptance themselves. Benton suggests that the seminary "would do well to provide opportunities for seminarians to experience relationships which are nonjudgmental, freeing, and deeply personal as a facilitation to becoming the kind of person who later seems to be an effective pastor."[104] Pastor Joan would have been helped with her later difficulties in dealing with normal sexual feelings had she been guided toward self-acceptance as a sexual being. Celibacy is one possible choice in handling sexuality. Properly understood, it is not a denial of sexuality. Joan was not helped to understand how sexuality is integrated in the pastoral role, rather than being in conflict with that role.

When pastors see themselves as persons and think about other people as persons, they are more likely to allow themselves to get personally involved with those they serve. Effective pastors seek to understand their parishioners' feelings as well as their own, and "perceive the possibility of personal growth in all interpersonal relationships."[105] The pastor who takes a more "professional" approach and stays personally aloof is less effective. The key seems to be the willingness of the pastor to be a person with those he or she serves. This is threatening to anyone who has not been reconciled to his or her own humanity.

How pastors think of themselves may relate to how they think about others in another way. Benton found that pastors who "perceive other people as human beings capable of seeing the right thing for them to do" and also capable of doing the right thing, are more effective than those "who see others as lacking the ability to find adequate solutions to their problems" and therefore in need of having the "answers supplied for them."[106] Some pastors have rather dependent personalities, as we have discussed.[107] Sometimes pastors confuse their own dependency needs with what others need. Pastor Joan expected herself to have an answer for the questions and problems of the people at First Community. While Joan did not think of it this way, when she saw herself as the parish pundit, or answer person, she was saying that, without her, her parishioners would not have been able to discover their own answers. Joan thereby took a parental position in relation to her counselees. Joan's assuming such a hierarchical role in relationship to the parishioners not only failed to draw the best from them, but also added needless stress to her ministry.

How pastors perceive their parishioners is important in another way. Effective pastors see those they serve as vital and responsive human beings, whose feelings and values are to be respected. Ineffective pastors tend to see "problems." Since most pastors, including Joan, think they are people oriented, they might not see themselves as relating to people as things. However, there is something very depersonalizing about speaking or thinking about a parishioner as "an alcoholic," or "a gossip," or a

"juvenile delinquent." Benton's research suggested that those
who typically think of parishioners in this "thingified" way were
less likely to be effective in their ministry.[108]

When people do have problems, Benton found that effective
pastors perceive their task to be a freeing of their parishioner
from judgment—the pastor's, the church's, and God's. Pastors
"who seek to control the behavior and/or feelings of [parishion-
ers] and who feel it is their duty to pronounce judgment" were
not nearly so effective as those who saw their task to free the parishioner "to discover and be aware of the various solutions to
their problems and to choose the solution [the parishioner] thinks
the best. . .in the situation."[109]

Benton concludes that the seminary needs to "concentrate
on the creation of a climate for emotional as well as intellectual
growth of the seminarian."[110] How the pastor *perceives* is more
important than what the pastor knows or does.[111] Pastoral attitudes, which are related to the pastor's assumptions, are of prime
importance. The Episcopal bishops appreciated in pastors "such
qualities as warmth, genuine interest in people, and. . .accep-
tance of others." The bishops also valued tolerance, flexibility,
and a pastor's willingness to listen to problems without imposing
his or her personal solution.[112] Such characteristics presuppose
a great deal of maturity, personal security, and love for people.

Becoming Mature in Christ

Such characteristics also grow out of a love for Christ. Losing
oneself in a role leads to a formal relationship with parishioners,
one which allows little freedom for either the ordained minister
or the congregational member to be fully and freely human. But
it is "for freedom that Christ has set us free." Finding oneself in
Christ opens a person to be who he or she is. "Finding oneself" is
more properly understood as having been found by God in
Christ. It is more than just knowing about Christ; it is a faith that
Christ has died *for me*.[113] In that ultimate security, those who
have been freed from fear become free for loving service. That is
what Christian maturity means.

Research such as Benton's challenges theological education,
which has often emphasized knowledge or content over interpersonal process, and the pastoral role over the pastoring person.

Benton is not suggesting that the pastor needs to know less. Rather, he is suggesting that a knowledge of theology and the skills of ministry will be of little value unless the person has learned to perceive with a pastoral love that affirms both self and other.

There also seems to be a correspondence between what Benton is saying and what we heard Reuter say about stress. The pastor needs to know when to take charge, and when to let go. This is true in relation to him or herself, and true in the pastoral relationship with parishioners. A real respect for oneself, one's strengths and limitations, enables this discernment in relation to oneself. An awareness of the limitations of others—but even more of their strengths—enables the pastor to provide a freeing ministry. Since we can give to others only what we ourselves have received, Benton appropriately advises the seminary to provide a framework for freeing the seminarian in deeply personal ways as a means of facilitating the person's becoming the kind of pastor who can manifest the meaning of grace in life.[114]

Pastor Joan had never experienced seminary the way we have described. She was therefore unprepared for a ministry that called for both more—and less. Joan thought that more courses and more skills would have better prepared her for First Community. In reality, more self-awareness and self-acceptance would have freed her to give more of herself and to have felt less responsible for providing what others need to learn to do—and sometimes are the only ones who can do—for themselves. The ministry of the laity can best be enabled by a pastor who has learned when to take charge and when to let go. The support of the people of God for one another rests on the willingness of that people to be genuine persons with each other, pastor and people, mutually dependent on a gracious God for life and for the only acceptance that ultimately matters. As one lets go of taking charge of one's salvation, there is all the more energy to take charge of those things which together, as the church, can be and need be done.

Pastor Joan did not leave First Community Church for several more years, nor did she leave the ministry. She chose to let go of her unrealistic need to be self-sufficient and self-denying. After a second meeting with Paul, she realized his needs were greater than she was prepared to handle, and she gently guided him to seek professional counseling. But she learned that she also needed some outside help and support, and Paul's courage was contagious. Joan sought out an older, married female pastor from a neighboring community, and soon the two of them formed a support group. In that setting Joan experienced the grace of acceptance and began to internalize the theology she had learned. She risked talking with her district head and learned that because so many new pastors felt the same way, the district was planning a seminar for pastors and spouses who had been in the parish fewer than five years. The seminar would not only retool but also provide time for personal and spiritual reflection. Joan went. The congregation Joan now serves is the richer for it, as is Joan, the man she later met and married, and the children they are now raising. Our Lord asks that we love others *as we love ourselves*. Joan's ministry is now oriented toward helping persons perceive what that means and what a difference it makes when such a witness is lived by those who have found themselves in Christ.

The Pastor
as a Feeling Person

Pastor John Faces Another Loss

John and his wife Ellen were just returning from visiting Ellen's grandmother. Grandma Miller was an alert 88-year-old who had finally lost her longtime battle with arthritis. She had not been able to walk without a walker for several years, and for the last six months it had been very uncomfortable for her to leave her chair for any time at all. Then, a bad flu virus had confined her to bed for several weeks, and the combination of her illness and her immobility had left her legs almost useless. The physician was suggesting that Ellen's mother needed to consider placing Grandma Miller in a home, because she would be requiring much more care, around the clock, than could be provided by any one family member. Ellen's mother was an only child, and Ellen and John lived five hours away. Although their youngest child had just left for college, Ellen was free from her nursery school work only on the weekends. A weekend, of course, was an impossible time for John to get away from the parish.

Ellen was lost in thought on the drive home. John was beginning to know firsthand some of the conflicts his parishioners felt when faced with similar problems and decisions. As he pulled into their driveway, John thought how good it was to be back home. The problems don't go away, but at least you're in your own world and troubles seem a little more manageable.

As John turned off the engine and opened the car door, he heard the telephone ringing. He felt for a moment like letting the persistent phone ring, but he had never been very good at that. Finally reaching the receiver, John heard the voice of a relieved Robert Barry. Rob Barry was a funeral director with whom John had a good working relationship. "I'm really glad I reached you," Rob said. "I'm afraid I have some bad news for you, John. Amanda Benz was taken to the emergency room this afternoon, and, well, she didn't make it. They think it was an aneurysm. There wasn't anything they could do. I'm sorry, John. I know how close the two of you were."

Amanda Benz. John remembered how instrumental she had been in his coming to Good Shepherd. She recognized the conflict he experienced about leaving Christ Lutheran, and her patience and consideration as chairperson of Good Shepherd's council had made it possible, finally, for him to say yes. Amanda's kind approach had not changed during all his seven years at Good Shepherd, in good times and in bad. When things were not going well in the parish or the parsonage, Amanda was always there with an encouraging word and an insightful suggestion. John and Ellen had been worried about their boy and the high school crowd he was in. Amanda's sharing of her experiences with her two now grown and happy sons had given John hope. Last year, when he failed to gain congregational approval to take an intern, something John had long hoped to do, Amanda had listened caringly and helped him put the vote in perspective. What would the council do without her? What would *he* do without her?

When Ellen entered the parsonage she found John just standing by the phone. "What's wrong, John?," she asked.

"Amanda," he said, "she's dead. I've got to go. The family is with Rob Barry now."

Ellen gasped with surprise at the news, but quickly regained her composure and nodded, understandingly. John went to change his shirt and freshen up a little after the long drive. As he prepared to leave for the funeral home, he thought of asking Ellen to call Dorothy Thaw, so she could get the Care Committee started. And Virginia. He hoped she hadn't left yet for vacation. Amanda had so loved to hear Virginia play the organ.

John was facing another loss. Perhaps "facing" is not exactly the right word. Facing carries with it the connotation of confronting something directly, personally, face to face. John felt unable to deal with Amanda's death in that simple and direct way. Rather than face Amanda's death, John, in his pastoral role as he understood it, had to "handle" her death. Her family was waiting. They not only would have immediate needs to which he must respond, but some special needs over the next few days which might be met by the Care Committee. Then, too, there was the funeral to plan.

The pastor must be a compassionate and comforting leader in times of grief and bereavement. Yet, the pastor as a feeling person is frequently grieving, too. John had grieved when he left his former parish to come to Good Shepherd. He grieved over his son in high school. He grieved over the loss of the internship vote. Recently, he grieved to see his last child leave home, even though John was happy to see his son enter a good college. He grieved with and for Ellen over Grandma Miller and the no-win decisions Ellen's parents were forced to make. Now John had lost a dear friend and supporter. Things at Good Shepherd would never be the same with Amanda gone, John was certain. His grief was real—but John was the pastor.

We shall now turn to what we know about the pastor as a feeling person. Are there some particular ways in which the role of the pastor inhibits the normal expression of emotion? Why is it so important that feelings be expressed? How can the pastor as a person most healthily and faithfully integrate personal feelings and professional ministry?

Learning Not to Feel

Like most seminarians and pastors, John is a "feeling" person. Studies of both seminarians and pastors suggest that more than two out of three pastors prefer to make important judgments on the basis of feelings and personal values, rather than on the basis of analysis and impersonal logic.[115] Many helping persons generally, but pastors in particular, share this personality profile.

How then can we account for the fact that many pastors, like John, find ways not to experience feelings? Why is it not uncommon to find pastors burying feelings behind the pastoral role? How does the pastor get the message that it is important to learn not to feel?

A look at the theological school environment may provide some perspective. While discussing depression in the seminary, Henri Nouwen observed that there are frustrations, emotional stresses, and identity concerns associated with each of "the three main areas of seminary formation": vocation, control, and competence.[116] I believe that these same formation issues can be useful in our attempt to understand how feelings may get lost in the pastoral role.

Seminary Formation and Feelings

Twenty years ago, when John decided to study for the ordained ministry, his entrance into seminary was shaped by the prevailing vocational images. He experienced pressure to control his emotions as well as his behavior. He also began to question how much emotion is compatible with professional competence. Each of these factors contributed in certain ways to John's learning not to feel.

In the seminary there is a strong induction into the role of the professional minister. A seminarian may perceive a need at least to try to fit the part that has been played by the pastoral models he or she most values. In John's day his denomination still maintained the tradition that clergy wear clerical garb. He had not been in the seminary many weeks before there was a vestment display. John proudly purchased his first black shirt with a clerical collar. He still remembers the day he first wore it. John's concern for outer apparel was symbolic of his inner need to measure up to what was expected of a theological student on the way to becoming a pastor.

The person preparing for ordained ministry is affected by vocational stereotypes not only about actions, but also about feelings. The second factor in the emotional life of the seminary is the emphasis on control. Without anyone ever saying it in so many words, John was quickly indoctrinated into what was considered appropriate and inappropriate emotional expression. It was appropriate for him to feel "concerned," but a seminarian (even less, the practicing pastor) "should not feel" overmuch anxiety ("Therefore I tell you, do not be anxious about your life. . ." [Matt. 6:25]). It was appropriate for John to feel righteous indignation, but a seminarian or pastor should not feel deep anger or resentment ("Lord, how often shall my brother sin against me, and I forgive him?" [Matt. 18:21]). It was appropriate to be alone and to value solitude, but pastors should not feel real loneliness or despair ("Lo, I am with you always. . ." [Matt. 28:20]). There were many other acceptable and unacceptable feelings that John learned mostly through his peers, often with only nonverbal cues. Most of his professors acted as if they, too, had learned the code, for he rarely saw one of them upset.

John paid a high price for adopting such a standard. One way to look at feelings is that feelings are neither good nor bad, although acting on those feelings may be either appropriate or inappropriate.[117] However, when feelings themselves are seen as good or bad, even conscious control of behavior is not enough. The very existence of "bad" feelings can lead to guilt and depression and fear of punishment by others or God.

Even though John rarely expressed undue anxiety or strong anger or real despair, he knew he sometimes felt those ways. When he did, he was unhappy with himself and he felt unfaithful. Mack Powell says that "Few other professional groups are [so] prone to guilt as the clergy."[118] Pastors are simply unable to meet their own high expectations and ideals, and these "unrealistic expectations are the central difficulty behind the guilt."[119] This guilt may be involved in some of the depression Nouwen was surprised to find in the seminary, and which some are surprised to find in the parish pastor. But the pastor is a person, and, as we have seen, there is always a price to be paid when personhood is lost in a role.

In addition to conforming to a vocational image, control of feelings can serve a personality need. The same studies that identify pastors as feeling persons have also pointed out their preference for an ordered and controlled life situation.[120] Feelings are perceived by some pastors as irrational, dangerous, and as disruptive or destructive. As we saw with Joan, strong aggressive and strong sexual feelings seem to be especially problematic for pastors. Feelings that are the most personally threatening are the ones we consciously or unconsciously try to control.[121]

John was raised in a rather repressed home environment. The only time he had heard his father raise his voice or seen him cry was when his father had been drinking. John's mother prized level-headed, common-sense thinking and, in reaction to her husband, clear-headed decision making. John's mother saw that he attended Sunday school, and his religious training seemed to confirm his fears about feelings. He began to think of feelings, especially strong feelings, as a danger not only to rationality but also to his soul. John believed he should control his emotions, and he searched the Bible to find specific guidance in how to exercise that control. What the Bible said became his safeguard, even though John's internal life never quite matched his external restraint. Of course, in using the Bible in this way, John gained a greater sense of control of his life situation, but he lost the flexibility and feeling of freedom the gospel promises. Reinforced in his control of feelings, rather than challenged to identify them and bring them to the surface, John could hardly grow in the integration of his feelings and his faith.

A seminary faculty can quite unintentionally add to the problems of persons like John. Seminary professors are persons too. Their very strengths can be their weakness. The person who chooses to spend years in preparation for ministry, and then additional years in graduate study in order to be qualified to teach in a theological school, has to have certain gifts. One of these is an analytical mind, a real asset in a doctoral program. However, those most likely to succeed in advanced study may be a bit overbalanced in the thinking dimension. The average seminarian and pastor tends to be less intellectually controlled and reflective than the average seminary professor, and pastors are typically more feeling oriented.[122] Unless a theological faculty person has made more than an intellectual effort to integrate feelings and faith, he or she may not recognize the struggles seminarians often have with their feelings.[123] If their teachers do not challenge seminarians to become aware of the relationship between their emotional life and their ministry, there will be little to offset the "closing off" effect of vocational stereotypes and the climate of control in a theological school.

Competence and Emotional Closeness

The third factor in the seminary which Nouwen found to be linked with emotional affect was competence. John felt a strong desire to be a professional. He wanted to be able to handle the demands of the pastoral role not only in the eyes of the church, but he also wanted to be recognized as a professional by the secular community. In the Western world, there are clear connotations of the word *professional*, and competence is one of them.

John's main interest was not counseling, but he wanted to have at least a basic proficiency as a counselor. In his one required seminary course in pastoral care, John was exposed to several counseling models, all of which emphasized the relationship between the counselor and the counselee. Among other things, John learned that the competent professional maintains enough distance between himself or herself and the patient or client to make it possible to be objective. When there is minimal training, it is quite possible to learn the dangers of counseling more thoroughly than the opportunities. John heard clearly the hazards of becoming emotionally involved with parishioners and overidentifying with their problems. He had a harder time integrating an appropriate professional objectivity with a real, personal presence with a hurting person.[124]

Seminaries expect an acceptable level of scholarship to mark the work of the person preparing for ordained ministry. In one research project, the most reliable predictors of academic success in the seminary were an applicant's college grade-point average and his or her performance on the Graduate Record Exam.[125] While this indicates that intelligence is needed to perform well in a seminary, it also suggests that the seminary may emphasize the academic at the expense of the professional. The academic is marked by abstract and theoretical thinking. The professional requires much closer integration with the real-life situation, and the real-life situation of human beings always includes feelings.

The competent student may not be a competent pastor. Bishops and judicatory heads of the church know this well. When asked how the seminary can do a better job preparing persons for ordained ministry, church officials express general satisfaction with the academic preparation of pastors, but they wonder whether somehow there can be more training in interpersonal relations.[126] Where people are involved, feelings are even more fundamental than facts. An academically trained pastor may be distinguished by knowledge of doctrine, but a professionally trained pastor must be competent both with theology and people.

Competence in pastoral care and counseling requires more than the mastery of facts and situations. However, pastors who have never been taught to learn from their own feelings often approach interpersonal situations as problems to be solved rather than people to be served. When John learned of Amanda's death, his actions were appropriate to his role. There were things that needed to be done, and John accepted the responsibility to do them. The time to work through his own feelings might need to be postponed. What we are asking is whether or not the pastor *ever* finds the "right time," and whether or not the pastor's training helps him or her to know just how important it is to find that time. Sensitivity to the feelings of others begins with sensitivity to one's own.

In the parish, vocational, control, and competence issues are as alive as Nouwen found them in the seminary. The additional problem is that they need to be exercised over against an even broader range of life experiences. A seminarian who experiences anxiety, anger, guilt, and other "negative" feelings in theological school will likely find that parish life is even more stressful. Moreover, those congregational frustrations often lead to even stronger feelings—and there is no graduation from them. If the pastor has a family and neglects that family for work, additional pressures and conflicts heighten these feelings. If one has learned that the competent, controlled professional should not feel a certain way, then periodically the pastor is likely to be as depressed as the seminarians Nouwen described.

Feelings are integral both to personal identity and to Christian faith. The integration of personal feelings and faith is crucial for effective and faithful ministry. However, before focusing on ministry, we shall first look at feelings in relation to identity. Is there something about ourselves that we come to know only when we are aware of our feelings and give them appropriate expression?

Feelings and Identity

It is not easy to lose someone or something that is very important to us. Sometimes the person or thing that is gone is so close to us that it seems like a part of us goes—or dies—too. We are never quite the same. John felt the truth of loss when Amanda died, because death has a way of breaking through our denial.

Death comes in many forms, and "little deaths" are around us all the time. Loss is at the heart of a stressful situation, and a significant stress or loss is a crisis. The transition from parish to parish or from one form of ministry to another is an often unrecognized loss or "death" experience, as John learned.[127] John also felt something of a "little death" when his son was having problems and when he lost his bid for an intern. Other pastors face a "little death" when they have serious health problems, like Pastor Tom, or when they face retirement (especially if they are not ready to retire), or when their marriages are in difficulty, or when everything in the new budget is passed except the proposed increase in the pastor's salary. A loss becomes significant when it is perceived as significant by the person who has experienced it.

The best known theorists in crisis and bereavement counseling have identified a similar pattern of feelings in reaction to loss.[128] (See diagram on page 92.)

A Pastor Faces a Loss

When John picked up the telephone and heard the funeral director's voice, he probably began to prepare himself to hear that someone had died. However, he did not expect it to be Amanda. He was understandably shocked to learn of her death. An almost reflexive "Oh, no!" is a common expression of denial.

After the initial reaction, there is a realization that the loss has really occurred. This is a time of heightened, even intense, emotional feeling. Amanda's family was likely either still in shock over her unexpected death, or early in the stage of realization when John arrived at the funeral home. The family's grief response over the next weeks and months probably will not follow

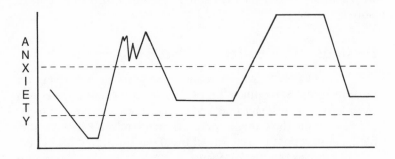

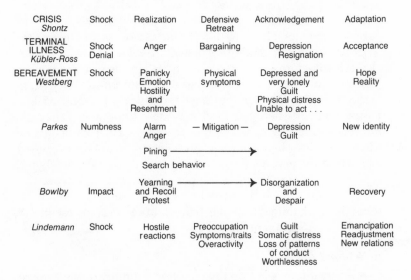

CRISIS *Shontz*	Shock	Realization	Defensive Retreat	Acknowledgement	Adaptation
TERMINAL ILLNESS *Kübler-Ross*	Shock Denial	Anger	Bargaining	Depression Resignation	Acceptance
BEREAVEMENT *Westberg*	Shock	Panicky Emotion Hostility and Resentment	Physical symptoms	Depressed and very lonely Guilt Physical distress Unable to act . . .	Hope Reality
Parkes	Numbness	Alarm Anger	— Mitigation —	Depression Guilt	New identity
		Pining ──────────────────►			
		Search behavior			
Bowlby	Impact	Yearning ──────────► and Recoil Protest		Disorganization and Despair	Recovery
Lindemann	Shock	Hostile reactions	Preoccupation Symptoms/traits Overactivity	Guilt Somatic distress Loss of patterns of conduct Worthlessness	Emancipation Readjustment New relations

the chart exactly, although during the grief process they will likely experience most of the feelings identified there at one time or another.[129]

But for John and other pastors in similar situations, the grief response is short-circuited. The shock is the same, but the realization mobilizes the pastor to action, rather than leads the pastor to his or her feelings. In a loss situation, the pastor's own grief can be very powerful, yet, as John saw it, the role required that his grief be "handled" rather than faced.

Facing Loss as a Whole Person

Henri Nouwen suggests that one price that may be paid for not being willing or being unable to express our own feelings is that it can cut us off from others.[130] I believe that, and we shall return to implications for ministry when we discuss feelings and faith. But here I want to stress that not attending to our own feelings cuts us off from ourselves. There is no healthy way for a whole person to respond to a loss except as a whole person.[131]

The pastor is a relating person, and because Amanda was personally close to him, John first felt her loss as a relational loss. When Amanda died, John's social world became a little smaller.

John is also a bodily being, and he was physically involved in his response to this loss situation. The shock of the news of someone close to us dying is often like a physical blow. An involuntary, sharp intake of breath is one sign of this trauma. Furthermore, John was physically tired. He had spent a stress-filled weekend with his wife and her family, and they had just driven five hours to get home. The call from Russell mobilized his remaining physical resources.

As a thinking person, John began to work on the arrangements that needed to be made. Were John less experienced, he might have genuinely wondered what to do or he may have worried about being able to meet the many, sometimes conflicting expectations produced by the death of a key member of the congregation.

As a believing person, John had to come to terms with the God-questions implicit in every loss situation. Why Amanda? Why now? What is the meaning and purpose of her death? If one of the ways God had been with him at Good Shepherd was through Amanda, what did it mean that Amanda was taken? Is God's promise of presence trustworthy?

The physical, mental, social, and spiritual do not stand in isolation. Each interacts with the other. At the telephone, John's sense of physical tiredness increased as he considered what needed to be done, even though he had not yet acted on any of those thoughts, and his tiredness affected not only *what* he thought about, but the *way* he was thinking.

John is somehow or other going to have to deal with his feelings if he is to be a whole person. John's personal history is important at this point. The loss of a loved person often resonates with other, earlier losses. How much "unfinished business" from past losses does John have? If the pastor does not recognize or deal with the many losses in pastoral ministry, that pastor becomes less whole as time goes on.

The danger, then, of pastors not dealing with their feelings is that they lose touch with what it is to be a person. But when feelings are faced openly and honestly, the pastor has the opportunity to become even more integrated as a person.

Feelings and Personal Identity

A major contribution to a (w)holistic understanding of emotion has been made by Robert Plutchik.[132] Plutchik defines *emotion* not simply as a feeling, but as a sequence of action triggered by something in the environment. The mind is involved in a cognitive appraisal of the situation. For example, if there is a perceived threat, the person may experience fear and run. Plutchik believes mental capacities evolved "largely in the service of the emotions."[133] He emphasizes that the emotional sequence enables a person to predict the future and so choose to take appropriate action.

Plutchik's work reminds the pastor that feelings involve the whole person. Our collective as well as our personal past and our probable future are all linked significantly to the way we deal with our emotions in the present. Plutchik suggests that if we learn the special language of our emotions, we can much more fully understand ourselves.[134] For the helping professions, like ministry, self-understanding is a key to understanding others.

Gaylin's emphases are somewhat different from Plutchik's, but he shares a similar (w)holistic orientation. Gaylin sees feelings not as an alternative to, but as integral to thinking and valuing. "Feelings. . .are testament to our capacity for choice and learning. Feelings are the instrument of rationality. . .we are capable of, and dependent on, using rational choice to decide our futures. Feelings become guides to that choice."[135] Gaylin divides feelings into three groups. Some feelings, such as anxiety and anger, guide our decisions toward individual and group survival.[136] Anxiety can be uncomfortable, but it can also keep us from crossing a street without looking. A second cluster of feelings warn us "that we are not achieving our goals, not serving our ends, or are depleting our resources."[137] Feeling upset, tired, or bored can lead us to pay attention to life-styles that need to be changed.[138] A third group of emotions includes being "moved" and experiencing pleasure and joy. These feelings "acknowledge the fact that [the] survival of the individual and group must have meaning beyond the mere fact of surviving. Life is to be enjoyed, not simply endured."[139]

Feelings can be ends in themselves, but they are better understood as leading beyond themselves to the fulfillment of human freedom and possibility. Linking feelings with freedom and choice, as Gaylin does, also helps the pastor realize that feelings are not peripheral. Without our feelings, we cannot think straight or act straight or be straight. Feelings are integral to our being who we are.

John cannot be all the person God created him to be without being in touch with his feelings about leaving one congregation for another or losing a valued friend and parishioner. John's decisions about what to do with his son and how to be most helpful to his wife and her family are dependent on John knowing how he feels, and John's using those feelings to guide him in offering his support. If John tries to act as if he were an objective bystander rather than an involved participant, he cannot help but come through as uncaring and aloof in his professional life and more like a pastor than a father or husband in his personal life. Our feelings assist us in making wiser choices, and it is in our choices that we most clearly express both our finite freedom and our ultimate values.

Another perspective on the relationship of feelings and personal identity comes from the developmental theory of Erik Erikson. Erikson discussed human development in terms of stages, each stage having a particular psychosocial task. In infancy, that task is to have a favorable balance of trust over mistrust. In the second year, the task is to achieve autonomy and to overcome immobilizing shame and doubt. Then it is the developing person's task to take initiative, overcoming guilt. During childhood, especially during the school years, industry (performance or mastery) is to have a favorable balance over feelings of inferiority. The adolescent's primary task is to achieve a stable identity and not fall into identity diffusion. In young adulthood, intimacy is to overcome isolation. Later, generativity—care for others—is the task, overcoming stagnation or a sense of going nowhere. Finally, the life-cycle task is to achieve integrity and, in the face of death, to affirm one's life, overcoming despair.

These life-cycle tasks are never fully completed. In every time of great stress, loss and crisis, a person reexperiences (recapitulates) his or her life cycle.[140] A truly critical situation brings out in us once more the basic, painful conflicts of our lifelong struggle toward identity. For example, when a spouse announces he or she wants a divorce, once again the rejected person has to try to overcome mistrust, shame, doubt, guilt, feelings of inferiority, loss of identity, a sense of isolation, stagnation, and despair. I believe this recapitulation is inevitable in any major crisis situation.[141] Furthermore, if we remember that a crisis is a real or anticipated loss experience related to the stress of change, then we can see that *any* meaningful change in a person's life can produce similar, although perhaps less intense, feelings.

The danger of a major crisis is that a person will be overwhelmed by these feelings and move toward illness. A loss situation presents the danger of personal disintegration. But the change is also a challenge. The loss provides an opportunity for a new, even healthier reintegration. By entering into the feelings surrounding loss, the person can become more whole.

Feelings and Pastoral Identity

Mistrust, doubt, guilt, despair—these and the other feelings are intensely painful. It is no wonder that many people, including pastors, want to deny or minimize a loss. We pastors can allow our role and our image of what a pastor *should* feel to shield us from such emotions, even when someone close dies, as John did with Amanda. In these cases, the pastoral role can lead us away from the kind of person-centered ministry we see in Jesus, who openly wept with those mourning the death of his friend Lazarus.

While pastors may knowingly suppress their feelings over great losses, they are more likely *unknowingly* to guard against their feelings when there are lesser losses. An example most pastors can identify with is the difficulty John had moving from Christ to Good Shepherd. Leaving a pastorate where one loves the people is a loss not only for the pastor, but also for the people.[142] John was in real conflict before deciding to leave. If he was a typical pastor, once that decision was made, he did not lead Christ congregation through the grieving process. He probably thought that to do so would have just stirred up the congregation and increased his own pain. When he arrived at Good Shepherd, that was not the time to deal with grief. On the contrary, had John looked grief-stricken or depressed, his new parishioners would have wondered whether he was happy with them. And John was pleased to be at Good Shepherd.

So John acted on some of his feelings, the "good" ones, while burying the rest. A little of himself died with his leaving Christ congregation. Because his loss was not fully integrated into his life, it was a death without a resurrection. But change is not only a danger, it is also an opportunity. Wholeness is not something we "have," but something we are called to and grow toward. By not risking the danger, John lost the opportunity to grow toward wholeness as a person. True identity for a Christian does call us into death, but the call promises that we shall also rise with Christ. When a pastor does not face feelings in a time of significant loss or change, he or she is denying the death without which there cannot be new life.

Feelings and Faith

When the emotional in the pastor's life is denied or ignored, the pastor is unable or unwilling to become involved. He or she is unable to enter "with the whole person into the painful situation."[143]

When John received the news of Amanda's death, he was called, in Nouwen's words, to be a "wounded healer" to her sons and their families.[144] To paraphrase Nouwen, ministry is not like medicine, where the physician exerts every effort to reduce discomfort. The minister intentionally deepens the pain. Amanda's sons bring their loss to John expecting not that John will take away their loss, but that he will understand their loss and feel with them. John's ministry is not to help them run away from their loss, or to minimize it by reminding them of all they still have. John is called initially to comfort, and later to help them perceive in the loss of their mother the fact of the human condition—the mortality which John and all others share with them.[145]

Ministry like this cannot happen if John personally maintains distance between himself and his feelings. "When we want to put our wounded selves in the service of others, we must consider the relationship between our professional and personal lives."[146] No one can be a "woundless" wounded healer. The pastor who denies or does not integrate into ministry his or her own feelings of hurt, or who is perceived as woundless, will also be perceived as "someone who has never been there."[147]

To "be there" is painful for a pastor, for more than ministry is at stake. The emotional is interrelated and interactive not only with the physical, mental, and social dimensions of life, but also with the spiritual. A pastor's retreat from his or her emotional center is therefore a retreat from his or her spiritual center. Our feelings in a loss situation are the feelings of death—the death of someone or something we love, and the death of the illusion of our own immortality.[148] Every significant loss invites us to face the fact of death in ourself. Feelings can be the pastor's guide to the as yet unresolved questions death raises in the mind and heart. Facing our feelings about death requires us to face the truth about ourselves.

But where there is no death, there is no possibility of resurrection. Christ invites the believer into the darkness, to a theology of the cross, apart from which the light of Christ can never really be experienced.[149] The theology of the cross gives depth to the theologies of hope and liberation. A deathless resurrection is like a woundless wounded healer. Ministry "does not allow people to live with illusions of immortality and wholeness. It keeps reminding others that they are mortal and broken." It is in this recognition, Nouwen goes on to say, that "liberation" begins.[150]

Death and Ministry

If a pastor is willing to enter into his or her own darkness, move carefully through the feelings surrounding loss in the parish and the parsonage, and get in touch with his or her vulnerability and powerlessness and mortality, then ministry can really happen. The first ministry is from God to the pastor. It is not to the pastor in his or her strength and righteousness and wholeness that Christ came and died. The gospel proclaims that for the weak and wounded, the sinful and the broken, Christ became obedient unto death. Grace means nothing if we do not need it. The pastor who follows his or her feelings into the dark knows the need and is gracefully met by the Christ.

The first ministry, then, is the ministry of God *to* the pastor. The second ministry is by God *through* the pastor. The liberated pastor carries the message of liberation. This does not mean that the pastor is merely a channel. *Through* the pastor means through the pastor's own history, the pastor's own life situation, and the pastor's body and mind and heart. When a pastor like John can honestly recognize that he is more like others than different from them, then his feelings can become guides to more faithful ministry.

It is helpful to reflect on one's experience and feelings in private, but talking through our memories out loud in the presence of a spouse or a trusted friend helps many persons to become aware of levels of feeling they had not realized were there. Pastoral support groups can help persons discover any "unfinished business" with the past. If it turns out that John really needs to reenter the darkness of his personal past in order to be free from it, then John's faith in the Christ who has gone before and meets us in the darkness can encourage him. A supportive person or group can be the embodiment of Christ's encouraging presence. If John is free from the past, then he is free for an even fuller ministry. The Christ *for* him can become the Christ *in* him, enabling John to encourage others entering the dark places of their lives.

Loneliness and Ministry

One of the darker experiences that often pervades a loss situation is the subsequent loneliness. The pastor has a special ministry to the lonely. This special ministry is related to the fact that many have noted the particular loneliness of the pastor as a set-apart person.[151] We have seen something of this in the story of Pastor Joan. Not in spite of the loneliness, but because of it, the pastor who has opened himself or herself to feelings is in an unusually good position to be sensitive to those experiencing the loneliness of loss and of life.

Nouwen sees this ministry not only as a special opportunity, but as a particular responsibility. "It is this wound which [he or she] is called to bind with more care and attention than others usually do."[152] The very weakness of the pastor therefore becomes a strength in ministry. But it can be a difficult ministry. "This is a very hard call. . .loneliness is a very painful wound which is easily subject to denial and neglect. But once the pain is accepted and understood, a denial is no longer necessary and ministry can become a healing service."[153]

It is through the willingness of the pastor to enter and reenter the darkness of his or her personal life that the fullness of the grace of God in Jesus Christ is an everyday, personal reality. The thoughts and feelings and needs aroused by the darkness become guides to the thoughts and feelings and needs of others in the darkness of their lives.[154] God's ministry through the pastor is a ministry of translucence: through the pastor comes the light of the Christ who has been met in the darkness, and this light lightens the darkness of others. If the pastor is unwilling to be in touch with important thoughts and feelings, those areas are opaque and unhelpful for others. The pastor is perceived as one "who has never been there." While there is risk in entering the most painful part of the pastor's personal life, the areas of particular weakness and vulnerability may lead to a ministry of special strength.

The Pastor
as a Relating Person

The Conflicts of Pastor Chris

Chris became the senior pastor of St. Peter's ten years ago. Since he was in his early fifties then, he saw St. Peter's as probably the parish from which he would retire. The way things were going, that retirement might come earlier than he had planned.

Chris was angry—furious would be more accurate. Ever since his assistant, Paul, had come to join the staff, there had been problems. During the interviews two years ago, Chris would never have imagined that the seemingly affable young man would have turned out to be so manipulative. The first clue came when Paul used certain key council members to put pressure on Chris to change their respective job descriptions. Paul wanted to preach more. Chris understood that changes in their working relationship would be inevitable as Paul matured, but his assistant had never really undertaken the outreach program as Chris had planned, and that is where the congregation needed an extra boost. Paul did preach well, though, and he found support for his bid for the restructuring of his role. What bothered Chris more than anything was Paul's going behind his back. Chris heard that, in the process, Paul had criticized some of Chris's priorities for St. Peter's. Paul had never discussed those concerns with Chris. Chris resented that.

What really infuriated Chris, however, was learning that last night Paul had made a thinly veiled sexual advance toward Ann Richards. Ann was a divorced mother of two who had asked Chris for some help adjusting to being single again. Chris had suggested that his assistant might be more up to date on the best resources. Paul began to counsel Ann several months ago. Just before Chris left the pastors' meeting earlier today, Ann had called and said she needed to discuss "something real important." She had come to Chris's office and uncomfortably, tearfully told Chris what had happened. She was not sure she had read Paul's intentions correctly. Chris listened supportively and without judgment, but inwardly he thought Ann had perceived Paul's invitation very accurately.

Chris knew that Paul and his wife Peggy had been having personal problems ever since Peggy had become pregnant again. Their second child was now about six months old. Chris had excused some of Paul's irritating behavior on the grounds that Paul was stressed at home. But this was too much! Chris could see his efforts to provide unified leadership at St. Peter's going right down the drain, and the last thing he wanted at this stage of his life was conflict.

Then there was one more concern. In an unguarded moment, during the early days after Paul came to be his assistant, Paul had said something about having had an argument with Peggy. Chris had confided to Paul that his own marriage had seen some pretty rough times, too. He did not tell Paul that those times continued, less with sharp words than sad neglect and the living of separate lives. But Chris had gone so far as to warn Paul that a pastor dare not mix his personal problems and pastoral counseling. Chris had never become sexually involved with a parishioner, but he had been tempted at times. Now it looked as if Paul had willfully gone ahead and abused the pastoral relationship. Partly because he had warned Paul, and partly because of his resentment over Paul's various manipulations, and partly because he had trusted Paul with such a personal part of himself, Chris was enraged at Paul for the predicament his assistant had put him in.

Chris did not know exactly what he was going to do. He knew he needed to calm down before doing anything, and he wished there were a way he could just do nothing for a while. Chris dreaded talking to Paul, which is why he had never mentioned what he had learned about Paul's behind-the-scenes operating with the council. If he said something to Paul, Paul would probably deny any inappropriate behavior. Then Chris would either be caught between Ann and Paul, or have to let someone else know about the problem. There was a pastoral relations committee, but if he went to the committee prematurely, it would be unfair to Paul—and Peggy. Then, too, Chris was not confident about his personal motives in light of Paul's recent criticism of him. If he tried to keep everything to himself, Ann would feel betrayed and he might be sitting on a time bomb. Chris had the ominous feeling that even though he had not personally done anything wrong, his own ministry at St. Peter's and his hopes for the future might be at stake.

Chris was feeling great stress as a result of his frustration with Paul and the pressure he felt to do something about it. He saw no way to avoid conflict, and conflict was something he had always tried to avoid. The pressure made him anxious, his frustration produced angry feelings, and the dangers of conflict made him afraid.[155] *This is normal feeling*

Chris's Story

Our physical, mental, and emotional reactions in any problematic situation have a "history," and Chris's personal history is very much involved in this situation. Chris was raised in a religious home, and his baptismal name, Christian, reflected his parents' hopes for him. He was a firstborn child, and his mother and father knew that the Old Testament spoke of dedicating the firstborn of all living things to the Lord. As he was being raised, Chris was protected as best his parents could from the harsher realities of life. They were a comfortable, middle-class family who never knew hunger firsthand. Chris learned that he could rely on his parents to meet all his basic needs and many of his wants. Chris was a "good" boy, and he learned that his behavior was valued by his parents. They commented proudly on his personality and his performance.

Chris's mother and father had an untroubled relationship, and they consciously kept any personal problems away from the children. Chris never really saw his parents fight, although, in later years and after his own marriage, he realized they must have had disagreements. His parents were active in church, and Chris had been a leader in his church youth group. After high school, where Chris was an honor student, he went on to a church-related college and then directly into the seminary. It seemed a very natural thing to do. He had never seriously regreted his decision for the ordained ministry.

Chris's marriage to Marilyn was something else. They had met during college, and she knew and approved of Chris's desire to go to the seminary. But they were very different persons, and the seminary put an unexpected strain on their relationship. Marilyn was much more expressive of her feelings than was Chris. Her personality had initially been one of the things that attracted Chris to her. However, while Chris's more quiet and passive temperament was reinforced in the seminary, Marilyn always felt judged for her outspokenness and emotionality. She kept getting subtle cues from Chris that he wished she were different, more charitable in her opinions, more "Christian."

In the early years of their marriage, Marilyn reacted against the constraints of the role of the pastor's wife. Chris did not really know how to resolve the problems with Marilyn, and he mostly tried to be understanding and patient. Once in a while he would become irritated, but he usually decided it was better not to say anything in anger, and generally the anger subsided enough to go on. Consequently, Chris and Marilyn's conflicts had never been worked through, although they reached an accommodation, with each of them leading their own lives in quite different ways.

Over the years, Marilyn had become involved with cultural groups in the communities where Chris served, and Chris did his best to be a dedicated and faithful churchman. From outward appearances, Chris and Marilyn seemed to have no serious problems. But Chris knew there were unfulfilled needs in his relationship with Marilyn, and Chris became alert to signs of similar dissatisfaction in the intimate relationships of others. There was something in the way Paul talked about his marital problems with Peggy that made Chris personally uneasy.

In all these ways, Chris's history was very much a part of his reaction to what Ann Richards told him about Paul. On the one hand, Chris was facing a crisis that now involved one parishioner, but threatened to involve the parish as a whole. On the other hand, what was alleged by Ann to have happened confronted Chris with the fact that pastors with marital problems are at special risk.[156] Chris could not completely avoid the painful, personal reminder.

Before turning to the personal dimensions of Chris's conflicts, let us consider the professional problem he faces. Staff ministries are often filled with stress.[157] The particular shape of the problems at St. Peter's may not be typical, but they do serve, in a magnified and intensified way, to point out tensions and feelings that are quite commonly found when pastors work together. Pastors are not given much training in working with another pastor, and struggles for position are more the rule than the exception.

Even though many pastors are uncomfortable thinking about their position in terms of power, power is involved. When Paul attempted to circumvent Chris on the preaching issue, he appealed to another source of power to lend weight to his bid for a changed role at St. Peter's. Power always involves authority issues, and usually has something to do with control.[158] As a result of Paul's manipulations, as Chris saw them, Chris felt less powerful, less the authority, and less in control. Then the situation with Ann Richards arose. How Chris responds to this crisis will probably affect the rest of his ministry at St. Peter's.

Chris shares with many pastors the failure to deal directly with issues of power and authority. There are a number of reasons why pastors may have an especially difficult time developing a healthy approach to power. One of the major reasons lies in a personality characteristic of many pastors that we have already mentioned: dependency. The more unhealthily dependent a pastor is as a person, the more difficulty he or she may have with acquiring and maintaining a sense of personal and pastoral authority. Chris's case helps us to consider the dangers of dependency.

The Dangers of Dependency

There are two clues to dependency that are helpful for pas-

tors to know. The first is how the pastor relates to authority figures, and the second is how that pastor handles feelings. The first
involves more of an historical perspective and requires that we recall our earlier discussion of Erik Erikson and the life cycle.

Dependency and Authority

When a pastor has a problem with his or her own power and
authority, it is very likely that he or she also has a problem relating
to the authority of others. Erikson's work helps us to realize that
the present reflects the past, and for persons to be independent
they must have worked out their earlier dependencies.

From the beginning of our lives, we are dependent on others. Chris was fortunate to have been born into a family where an
infant was wanted and nurtured. His dependency needs were
met. Around the second year of his life, he began to be more independent and to make his initial efforts to stand on his own two
feet. Of course, at the same time he did not want to lose his parents' love and care. This "letting go while holding on" was symbolic of the way in which dependency and independence would
be an important point and counterpoint throughout Chris's life.
To know how a pastor has learned to balance his or her needs for
dependence and for independence is crucial for understanding
that pastor as a person. The balance will also be critical for understanding the way that pastor will relate to others in ministry.

We remember that Chris was sheltered as a child. Sometimes
persons who have grown up under the protection and power of
loved, respected, strong adults never fully realize their own personal power. Deep inside, they need others—their presence, their
approval—in order to feel good about themselves. This is often
the case with the compliant child, who may, perhaps unconsciously, continue through life to look for someone or something
to help him or her to "make it." That some of these persons would
be attracted to the ordained ministry, which provides a strong
family-like framework and the promise of much approval, is really not surprising. Chris seems to have had many of these characteristics.

Paul seems to relate to authority differently from Chris. As
Chris tends toward dependency, Paul seems to be the independent type. But Paul may not be so independent as he appears. An-

other form of dependence is what we see in the reactive or rebellious child and adolescent (or adult), the one who says no not just to establish identity, but who needs to continue to say no to others or to social conventions in order to be somebody. We usually do not perceive the dependency in this kind of behavior, as it may appear so independent, even antisocial.

However, let us think about compliance. When someone conforms or is submissive, that person conforms to or submits to or complies with someone or something. The person's behavior is not independent; it is very much dependent on someone (a powerful person) or something (a compelling rule or value). Similarly, the reactive or rebellious is not isolated action, but reaction to or rebellion against someone or something. Therefore, in both submissive compliance and rebellious reaction there is no real independence.[159] There is some tie, some dependency, that underlies the giving in or the fighting back. In his analysis of "disobedient dependence" Richard Sennett emphasizes how rebelling establishes even stronger ties with whatever or whomever a dependent person is struggling against.[160] Furthermore, Sennett links power and authority when he says: "Our need for authority relates to our desire for guidance, security, and stability. . . . The bond of authority is built of images of strength and weakness; it is the emotional expression of power."[161]

The nonconformist may be every bit as closely tied to authority, but in a reactive rather than an adaptive way.[162] Paul and Chris may have different ways of expressing dependency, one more recognizably dependent and the other counterdependent, but the one may be no less dependent than the other. The first clue to dependency lies in the way the pastor relates to authority. Neither a too ready compliance nor a near-automatic reaction suggests an independent person. No one is completely dependent or completely independent. As Erickson points out, it is the balance that is important. Paul's situation is less certain, but, like most pastors, Chris clearly seems to be overbalanced in the direction of dependency.[163]

Dependency and Anger

While history is one clue to dependency, a second clue is more experiential and has to do with how a pastor handles his or her feelings. In Chris's case, we have a good example in his anger. Before pursuing how Chris's angry feelings are linked with dependency issues, we must first note that anger is not a simple word to use when describing a person's feelings. *Anger* has the same root as *anguish*.[164] Rather than being seen as a primary emotion, anger is sometimes viewed as the way we may feel when we are afraid (fear leading not to flight but to fight) or when we have been hurt ("I'm angry at her for leaving me!").[165] Sometimes persons feel anger when they are really suppressing guilt. Directing strong, negative emotions outward may be more comfortable than having them inside oneself. *Anger* then, may not represent a single emotion.

In this situation with Paul, what suggests dependency is not the fact that Chris feels angry; that is understandable. What indicates dependency is where Chris locates the responsibility for his anger. Chris sees the responsibility for his anger to be outside himself—in Paul. The usual way to say it is that Paul "made" Chris angry. The truth is that no one can feel for us, and no one can *make* us experience a feeling.[166] Chris is angry, but the anger is his, and the responsibility for what Chris does with his anger is Chris's too.

The extent to which we see our problems as residing in someone else suggests our degree of dependence on others. If others can *make* me feel happy or sad, calm or angry, loved or unloved, acceptable or unacceptable, worthwhile or not worthwhile, then I am really dependent on those others. Power is thought to arise from the situation of unfulfilled needs, and power is given to those who can fulfill those needs. Another way to say this is that "power resides in dependency."[167] When we "give away" to someone else the ability to make us feel a certain way, then we give away our personal power over our own lives. In doing that, we also lose touch with our personal responsibility for our thoughts, feelings, and behavior.

Chris is in a muddle because he does not know what to do. He is not certain how to keep what he has learned about Paul from erupting into a conflict that would threaten the parish and perhaps his own ministry. In addition, Chris has some resentment about the way Paul has treated him, and he feels afraid and vulnerable because his relationship with Marilyn is not what it appears to be. Chris is afraid to act, and afraid not to act, and he senses that he cannot sit very long on what he knows. What are the dangers of Chris's dependency in this situation?

Dependency and Personal Integrity

The first danger is that dependency threatens Chris's integrity as a person. By *integrity*, I do not mean moral integrity. Chris is a moral man, an ethical professional. The integrity that is endangered is Chris's wholeness as a bodily, thinking, feeling, relating, and believing person. Unhealthy dependencies, as we have suggested, begin early in life when a person not only feels small, but physically *is* small. Originally, we were dependent on others for our very survival. Later, survival was less tenuous, and dependency was linked with the need for security.[168] In certain ways, the overly dependent person may never feel physically quite grown up, never quite big enough to take care of himself or herself. Consequently, there may be special problems with "body image" in dependent individuals, as if the inner inadequacies actually took physical form. None of this, of course, has anything to do with actual body build. Chris was a physically large man, but that did not stop him from being much more dependent on others than another pastor might have been. In dealing with Paul, Chris felt "small."

Dependency is in many ways a matter of the mind, and Chris had learned to think of himself as worthy and acceptable only when someone else pronounced the words. He had not internalized the message, and so he was dependent on others to tell him who he was and how he was doing. One of the reasons he loved church work was that it gave him the opportunity to proclaim again and again the words of God's acceptance, but Chris never quite believed that those words were really meant for him personally. He had been called to a position of power, but Chris experienced little power as a person, for he had given so much of it away.

Nowhere was this more true than in the emotional area. Chris's anger was not really integrated into his life. He saw his angry feelings caused by what was outside, and so for him to feel different, something outside had to change. Chris simply did not identify intense emotional experience as being his choice and his responsibility.

The primary way Chris's dependence was expressed was in his relationships. When we discussed the liberation of Pastor Joan, we saw how the role expectations of pastors are many and varied. Among them is the expectation that the pastor will provide authoritative leadership. Since there are many notions of what authoritative leadership in any given situation might be, pastors are understandably distressed if they attempt to live up to all of those diverse expectations.[169] Whenever there is a question about pastoral misconduct, feelings are strong and opinions are divided. Since Chris had strong dependencies, his need to meet everybody else's need in this situation frightened him. His fear of failing to be able to meet all those needs was a factor in his holding back as long as he could.

One of Chris's most unsettling realizations was that God's way of reconciling this situation might not completely meet *anybody's* expectations, even his own. Chris was never more stressed than when he realized that God's call was leading him in a direction psychologically most difficult for him to go. He feared that this might be one of those times. Physically, mentally, emotionally, socially, and spiritually, Chris was confronted by his dependency and the threat to his personal integrity that it posed.

Dependency and Pastoral Ministry

But Chris is not functioning in this situation only as a person. He is also a pastor. A second danger of dependency is that the pastor may be so concerned about how things look that he or she will settle for the *appearance* of a resolution. Chris does not have much of a feeling of power in this situation. He feels frustrated and trapped by Paul and the circumstances. Chris's personal history gives us reason to suspect that one of his concerns is how these things will look to the parishioners, if and when they become aware of what has happened. Chris had settled for appearances in his marriage. He also settled for appearances when he publically witnessed to the unity of leadership at St. Peter's, even though he knew about some of Paul's private maneuvering and did not confront him about it. In this counseling situation, let's assume that Paul in fact did make a pass at Ann. If Paul denies and dismisses Ann's complaint, and Ann begins to doubt her perception and feel guilty about having said something to Chris, Chris's need to have things look good may motivate him to pass the whole matter off as a misunderstanding, even though a part of him is not convinced. Dependency, then, may show itself as a concern for things to look good, and this kind of dependency can endanger the integrity of any ministry.

Dependency and Fear of Loss

The third danger of dependency is that it locks a pastor into a life-style and ministerial style that is self-perpetuating. The dependent pastor does not welcome change because change always involves a loss, and it is possible that one of the losses will be the person or the thing depended on. Chris has a vested interest in the status quo. He knows what to expect from Marilyn. Even though he might have wished for more from his marriage, he has learned to value certain consistencies in the relationship. To try to change things would rock the stability of the marriage and threaten his security. After survival, the dependent person most longs for security. But the very security that offers protection from the outside also, from the inside, can feel like a prison. As a result, a dependent person rarely feels really free. There is rather a feeling of "ought" and "should" and "have to" about life and relationships, and a somewhat compulsive quality to the pastor's way of going about ministry.

One of the most compelling "shoulds" for the dependent pastor is to avoid conflict. Conflict is not only threatening because of the emotions that may be involved, but because conflict may lead to change, and change leads to a loss. When Chris considers what might happen if the problem with Paul becomes known in the parish, his fantasies almost always turn to the polarization of the congregation, with Chris caught in between. Theoretically, Chris might be able to understand that a conflict can surface tensions that need to be expressed in order for the air to be cleared, but emotionally Chris only feels the concern that things will get out of control.

A dependent person will have trouble with the negative emotions involved in a conflict situation, and the overly dependent pastor will have an equally difficult time with growth—personal or professional. Growth occurs in critical steps where there is both risk and vulnerability. Something has to be left behind in order for something new to happen. As Tillich put it, the actual must be sacrificed in order to attain the possible.[170] When a pastor too carefully protects himself or herself against loss, he or she loses the possibility of growth.

While our primary focus has been on the way Chris's dependencies affected his personal and pastoral ministry in the parish, the fear of loss affects not only ministry, but also a pastor's close interpersonal relationships. A look inside the parsonage at St. Peter's helps us to understand some of the pressures married pastors face in this day when the "new morality" is no longer so new.

The Not-so-new Morality

When Chris and Marilyn met in college, Chris was already making plans to enter the seminary. Marilyn was an art major, with a flair for dramatics. In fact, Marilyn had a flair for just about everything. She was an active member of a sorority, a free spirit well-liked by her "sisters."

Marilyn was a charming and entertaining conversationalist, frequently the life of a party, which she loved. She really knew how to enjoy the moment. Where she got her energy nobody knew. She could be rehearsing for a play, working on a major art project, and studying for exams, and still she was ready at a moment's notice to help plan an end of the quarter celebration or take an extra shift at the campus crisis center, where she was a volunteer on the community hotline.

Chris was very much attracted to Marilyn's extroverted approach to life and her ease around people. He liked people, too, but he had always been a little shy, especially around people he did not know well. Marilyn's light-hearted optimism also complemented his more serious nature.

Marilyn saw in Chris a challenge. He had such a sense of responsibility and such a need to take care of others that most of his time was spent preparing for the future when he could be a pastor. Marilyn felt sure she could convince Chris to live more for the day. She counted it a major victory when she was able to persuade

Chris to ignore the campus curfew or set aside the books to attend a play in a nearby city.

Underneath his sober side, Marilyn detected Chris's warmth and steadiness, which she valued and admired. She knew that she could rely on Chris and that there would be stability with him, something she had missed while growing up in a single-parent family. Chris was committed to institutions like the family and the church, and she knew as a husband that he would be a pillar of strength. While some of her friends wondered whether they might not be too different, Marilyn was certain that Chris was the man for her. She was a little concerned about being a pastor's wife, but Chris convinced her that parish life could be exciting and that he had been told that it was becoming acceptable for clergy wives to pursue their interests in activities and work outside the home.

A Marriage Model

During their nearly 40 years of married life, Chris and Marilyn had many hurdles to overcome. It is predictable that couples who stay together for any length of time will have to negotiate their relationship in a number of crucial areas. One way to conceptualize any marital relationship is by combining the (w)holistic model with current research on intimate relationships.[171]

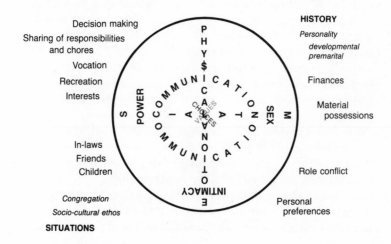

While this model can be used in situations where there is no present marital problem, the model can also provide an easily remembered framework for considering the primary symptoms of marital breakdown.[172] In no particular order, the physical dimension reminds us that there can be conflicts over the use of material resources (finances, possessions). Moving from physical to mental, there may be problems with sex, sex-role conflicts, and personal preferences. Physical sex and gender tensions are frequently related to problems with emotional intimacy. The social dimension reminds us of the power issues involved in every relationship, often seen in the ways a couple makes decisions and shares responsibility. Power is wielded particularly in decisions about finances, intimacy, and sex. It is also important in the social area to note what and how decisions are made concerning children, in-laws, friends, chores, interests, or recreation. All these dimensions interrelate and interact, as the (w)holistic model graphically shows, and are evident in the content and quality of communication a couple establishes. Each potential problem area is related not only to each other, but also to the underlying individual and relational values that reflect spiritual depth.

History is an important dynamic in marriage. The personality each partner brings to the marital union is relevant history, as are the things about marriage the husband and wife learned in their respective families of origin. When couples have a problem with in-laws, there is always this past as well as a present tense. The history of the relationship since the marriage helps identify previous areas of stress and the way in which the conflicts that have arisen have been resolved.

The current life situation of the couple is also a critical factor in marital harmony or disharmony. Marriage is a system, and a systems approach is very helpful.[173] To the potential systemic problems already listed under the social dimension, we must add the couple's employment. Vocational issues are often critical factors in marriage problems, and this may be especially true for ordained ministers. Of course, for parish pastors and spouses the life situation always includes the congregation.

Finally, the model applied to marriage reminds us to reflect on the marriage from the perspective of choices. There are two persons with a unique past personal and interpersonal history.

They are experiencing problems in their present life situation. How does each choose to face the future—as an individual no longer wanting to be married, as a married person essentially living as a single, or as a couple. If the choice is to face the future as a couple, is it simply to remain together, or is it also to grow personally and as a couple through the relational conflict and pain?

With the rising incidence of divorce and marital problems in the parish, it may be instructive to point out some potential problem areas Chris and Marilyn faced.[174] Chris and Marilyn's personality types were selected because Chris has characteristics shared by many pastors.[175] There is also a high frequency of marriages between persons having the personality types of Marilyn and Chris.[176]

A Pastor's Marital History

Chris was a product of a close-knit family where there were clear expectations, goals, and hopes. Chris was oriented to a life of service, and he wanted to use his gifts within the church where he thought he could do the most good. He knew he could overcome his natural timidity, and the role of the pastor would help him to meet the public demands of that office.

Marilyn, on the other hand, grew up without a father and was much attracted to Chris's strength and the stability he represented. She had learned to meet her needs by remaining open and responding flexibly, even spontaneously, to the immediate situation. Sometimes she felt the need of an anchor, and Chris provided that. At times, Chris wanted a little relief from the seriousness of life, and Marilyn offered that.

Marilyn was much more extraverted than Chris, although he cared for people every bit as much. It is not uncommon for extraverts and introverts to be attracted to each other. It is also not uncommon for them to have marital problems because of their different orientation.[177] Marilyn tended to need a lot of verbal interaction. Her thinking was clarified by her speaking her thoughts out loud. Chris did a lot of his processing in his head.[178] After a while, Marilyn felt that Chris was not so interested in her as he had once seemed. Very probably, Chris had not changed. Marilyn's active social life may have masked the fact that Chris simply had different communication needs than she. Their problem with communication had never been fully resolved. It was the cause of many of the other problems they faced over the years.

Communication breakdowns usually affect decision-making processes. Decisions are based on what is important to a person. Marilyn was oriented to the present and to the enjoyment of the present. Chris was oriented to the future, and motivated to give up the satisfactions of the present for the future. It is not hard to see how Chris and Marilyn would have disagreements over the use of money, both on what to spend it on and how much to spend. Chris wondered at times just how responsible Marilyn was, disinterested as she was in planning or saving for the future. Marilyn questioned the priorities of Chris's work ethic and concern for what might happen. She began to resent the way her interests and her desire for recreation were progressively squeezed out on the grounds of both money and time. Tomorrow might never come.

Eventually, Marilyn learned that she needed to expand her circles of friends. When Chris was in seminary, Marilyn realized that the theological school environment attracted many more people who thought like Chris than people who shared her values. She and some other seminary wives who enjoyed the arts developed a clique and followed their interests as opportunities arose. Marilyn really missed these women when she and Chris left school for his first parish. When Chris and Marilyn realized that they were not going to have any children, Marilyn put her creative energy into community theater and other cultural projects. Her circle of friends ranged far beyond the parish. Chris sometimes felt Marilyn was not involved in the congregation as much as she should be, but Marilyn resisted his efforts to guide her activities. Almost as a compensation, Chris put all the more time and effort into his ministry. In time, it was almost as if he and his wife were heading their separate ways. They spoke less and less about what was going on in the congregation. They spoke less about everything. As their intimacy decreased, their sex life became more perfunctory and their interest declined. "Perhaps," Chris once pondered, "it's because we're getting older."

During the earlier years of their marriage, divorce was not so common. Marilyn knew how hard her mother had struggled on her own. Later, with the onset of the "new morality," more and more of her acquaintances left their marriages. Marilyn thought about it, too. But she really cared for Chris and respected him for all that he stood for. She knew the effect a divorce could have on his ministry, and she would not hurt him for the world. As far as Chris was concerned, once married, always married. He had been attracted by another woman once or twice, but even if they had not been parishioners, he would not have been able to live with himself had he acted on such impulses. That is what he did not understand about Paul.

The pastor and spouse live under some special situational stresses. Chris's personality characteristics would have been a problem for Marilyn, even if Chris had not gone into the ministry.[179] However, some of the most problematic traits were very heavily reinforced by his pastoral role, for example, his work ethic. Marilyn and Chris needed to negotiate a balance between hard work and healthy recreation. Life cannot be all play; neither can it be all work. Yet Chris received few challenges from parishioners (or district officials) over his 60-hour work week.[180] Instead, he heard words like "dedicated" and "a true pastor."

If anyone was suspect, it was Marilyn. Many wives of pastors have not had Marilyn's courage to withstand the pressures of the parish to conform. Marilyn decided to live her own life, disappointed that it had to be that way. Those wives who conform to the pressure are more likely to feel resentment, not only against the parish but also toward their husbands. It remains to be seen how spouses of female pastors will handle these pressures and problems. Perhaps a different set of problems will arise.

The Challenge of Marital Conflict

When persons have problems in a relationship, and they realize that there are problems, they can do one of three things about it. First, they can protect themselves from the potential pain. This is what happens when a couple denies the existence of difficulty or, if denial is impossible, ignore it or minimize it or avoid the problem. This is basically a passive stance. It is likely to be taken by a dependent person who fears change. As we have seen, Chris was this kind of person. He feared losing what he had, and so hoped that by patience and perseverance everything would turn out all right. Usually things do not work out very well with a passive approach, although the couple may stay together.

A second thing people with relational problems do is more action oriented. Perhaps Paul felt neglected and ignored at home after the birth of the second child. Ann Richards felt some guilt that something she did could have been misinterpreted by Paul. However, Ann really may have had little to do with what happened. She may have just chanced to be the most attractive counselee Paul was seeing precisely at the time he was feeling most displaced at home. Paul could have been consciously angry at Peggy and simply not have realized the way in which that might affect him in close, interpersonal relationships with other females. In retrospect, Paul may even have wondered how things got so out of hand. Of course, Paul could also be a person with much less integrity than Chris, who knew very well what he was suggesting and had it backfire. However, my experience in counseling pastors in sex-related areas leads me to believe that most pastors are sincere men and women who are as genuinely shocked that they had a sexual problem as the parishioners who learn about it.

There is a third alternative to actively protecting oneself from the pain of a problem, or actively and unwisely "acting out" the problem. A person can choose to admit the presence of a problem and commit himself or herself to deal with it. This is a choice that takes a great deal of courage, especially for persons who live the highly visible life of pastors and their spouses.

The Church and Clergy Marriage

While no one can make such a personal confession and commitment for us (not even our spouse), the institutional church can help those in ordained ministry see a choice to seek marital counseling as a viable alternative. Marilyn and Chris may have been helped toward a much happier life together had there been adequate encouragement and support from the leadership of their church early in their marriage, or at critical turning points along the way—if they had been willing to accept that help.

One of those turning points came in seminary. In Protestant seminaries, a high percentage of students are married when they enter school or become married during the seminary years. Yet few seminaries have any intentional program for working with engaged or married seminary couples. While Marriage Encounter is promoted in many denominations, an experience designed to make a good marriage better, there are few analogous efforts specifically designed for the pastor and spouse in training for the parish. This is not so surprising when we realize that the seminarian probably has not even had a required course in premarital or marriage and family counseling. The seminarian may therefore have neither a theoretical nor an experiential base for dealing with personal problems in his or her own marriage and family. Since the seminary serves the church, it may take the voice of the church to help those preparing persons for ministry to realize the opportunity that is lost when preventive care for parsonage couples and families receives such low priority.

However, the church has opportunities that can be provided after seminary that will always need to be offered, because life in the parsonage can never be fully anticipated by training in the seminary. Some denominations have begun to schedule marital growth experiences, and pastoral retreats are now, at times, opened to spouses and families, with appropriate educational offerings that serve a preventive function.[181] The church can also consider marking more closely anniversaries and special events in the marital and family life of pastors and spouses. What is needed here is not a card or a letter, but an invitation to join others in a time away—a time of renewal provided by the church for the pastor and spouse. This is no easy task with the large number of working spouses, male and female. But it is a way of saying that the pressures on pastoral marriages are great, and the church cares enough to be supportive. Of course, some of the most troubled marital partners may never accept such invitations. Just as the pastor must make calls on those who do not accept the invitation to worship, so judicatories need to consider both pastoral calling on pastors and the provision of additional counseling resources that are competent and confidential—preferably apart from a superintendent's or bishop's supervision.[182]

Even with all that the church can do, it still is up to the individual pastor and spouse or family member to accept the responsibility to seek help when help is needed. No one can help someone who has not chosen to be helped. The pastor who is more likely to take this kind of personal responsibility is the pastor who has come to terms with the authority issues in his or her life. For those pastors who have a history of giving their personal power away, it is a matter of their learning to recover their authority, and of their recognizing what true authority involves.

The Recovery of Authority

Identity and authority are closely interrelated. There is really no way to talk about identity without talking about authority. *Authority* has the same English root as the word *author*.[183] An author originates or makes, and an authority is a powerful and decisive author, on whose pronouncements one can depend. To reflect on personal identity is to speak about personal authority, just as to discuss pastoral authority requires that we consider pastoral identity.[184] How interrelated the issues of personal and pastoral identity and authority are will become even more apparent as we consider further the conflicts of Pastor Chris.

Personal and Pastoral Authority

Chris is in a predicament at St. Peter's. An actual or potential conflict situation in the parish or in the parsonage characteristically leaves Chris feeling powerless, without authority. When he feels frustrated in this way, he feels diminished as a pastor and as a person.

Of course Chris *has* authority. In the parish, he is the senior pastor. He has been called to exercise leadership in the congregation, to *be* an authority. Chris was called to preach the Word of God and administer the sacraments, to lead God's people in worship, and in their translating their worship to everyday witness to Jesus the Christ. That is real authority, power, and responsibility.

Yet, being called to an office where authority is conveyed by virtue of the position is not the same thing as experiencing oneself as an authority.[185] There are two reasons for this breakdown in authority. One of the continuing problems in pastoral ministry is that there is an attribution of pastoral authority (and responsibility) not only in Word and sacrament, but in *all* areas of parish life, from alb alterations to photocopying, and all the congregational activities in between. However, there is no real pastoral power to legitimate that kind of comprehensive authority.[186]

There can be no actual authority without power, and feeling responsible for authority without power can lead only to frustration and guilt.

The second way in which authority breaks down is when there is power but it is not recognized or not claimed. Chris's feeling of powerlessness does not necessarily mean he was without power. It may simply have meant that he was unable to identify and claim the authority that was his. John Fletcher insightfully observed that there are three stages clergy must grow through on the way to authentic ministry: a stage in which personal strength is tested, a stage during which professional authenticity is developed, and a stage in which the ordained and lay discover their particular ministries.[187] If the pastor avoids the personal pain of being discovered as a person, and the congregation is not strong enough to push the testing, "a pattern of permanent avoidance can set in," reminiscent of "marriages that persist but do not live."[188]

From what we have seen in Chris, there is every possibility that the first critical stage of personal strength and authenticity had been successfully avoided during his pastorate at St. Peter's, just as he had avoided facing the underlying problems in his marriage. If Chris did not claim his authority as a person, husband, and pastor, this may not have been because of the absence of power, but the failure of courage. Fletcher points out that "nothing of significance happens in a [comfortable but dying] congregation until there is a recognition by the clergyperson and the leadership of the congregation that 'something is wrong.' What the 'something' is can be discovered only if there is enough personal strength in the clergyperson to pay attention to the trouble and ask for help. . .as long as pain is avoided, growth is arrested."[189]

"Personal strength" requires something quite different from what Chris might imagine. Chris's history from childhood on emphasized strength as being good, in control, and responsible. Even though he was dependent on others, Chris probably was not aware of his need for others nearly as much as he was aware of his being needed by them. His ready willingness to respond in a helping way to anyone who asked him was seen by others as strength, and this reinforced Chris's idea that to be strong meant to be able to take charge and do something for somebody. However, in the situation with Paul, to take charge and use his power meant the probability of conflict.

Conflict, for Chris, was something he wanted to avoid. Like many pastors, Chris identified conflict with weakness and failure.[190] Conflict meant disruption and change, a potential loss situation. Conflict was a threat to the familiar, making the world less secure. Some of the personality characteristics we have found in Chris are shared by the vast majority of clergy. Among those are the appreciation for an orderly, reasonably predictable environment.[191] When the need for order is too strong and being in control is too important, conflict is avoided, because change is not seen as a challenge, but only as a danger. Rather than seeing the opportunities inherent in conflict, the many pastors who share Chris's perspective perceive only a threat to what they have accomplished. If they do anything at all during such a critical time, it is more likely to be an attempt to get and keep things under control.[192]

Unfortunately, the pastor who identifies conflict with a failure of strength, and therefore avoids conflict, may never know what real strength is. The Bible does not lead us away from conflict, for "conflict is central to Christian experience and doctrine."[193] Rather than avoiding conflict, the Christian is guided into it and through it. Paradoxically, the crisis of conflict is not overcome by a believer's *strength*, but through the believer's *weakness*. By his avoidance of conflict and his insistence on being seen as strong, as he understood strength, Chris never could reach what Fletcher calls "professional authenticity," that stage where pastoral persons "grow beyond the need for omnipotence to acknowledge dependence on God as the authentic source of strength."[194]

The key to the recovery of personal power and pastoral authority therefore involves a change in perspective. Real authority does involve dependence, but it is not the dependence of others on the pastor and the pastor's reciprocal dependence on being needed. Real authority is based on the absolute dependence the pastor has on the Author of life. Fletcher's authentication process is completed not in the separation of the authoritative pastor from a dependent laity, but in the pastors "interpreting the problem as spiritual in nature, sharing openly the dilemma and accepting spiritual guidance from the laity who understand only too well what has happened. The essence of the religious experience is the acknowledgment of our ultimate dependence. Not until the clergyperson's own experience in the congregation reveals the quality of living dependently on God, rather than the congregation living dependently on the leader, is the crisis transcended."[195] The true interdependence of pastor and laity is realized in their mutual acceptance of their common dependence on God.

Whether dealing with a particularly thorny problem in the parish or a complicated relationship in the parsonage, a pastor has to come to terms with his or her strengths and limitations as a person. What Chris can or should do about his marriage or about the parish problem is not so much the point as how Chris might allow these crises, one chronic and one acute, to lead him to recover his identity and his authority. Absolute dependence on the God we know in Christ Jesus will strengthen the pastor for the hard work of reconciliation, which is the appropriate exercise of personal and pastoral power. The *how* of that reconciling work may not be known by Chris until he acknowledges his weakness and need for strength beyond himself. The confidence a pastor gains from turning to the Author of life is the awareness that he is only a prayer away. That is a great comfort as we write the next page of our life story.

For Chris to handle his relational crises any differently than he has in the past is a matter of choice. His personal history suggests that he may not perceive the many options that are available in his present life situation. But the power of God to transcend history and the situation has been made known to us in the gospel. In the death and resurrection of Jesus, we have the paradigm of the Christian's life as a choosing person. Jesus invited us to take up our cross daily and follow him. The cross was for Jesus a choice, and so it is for the pastor as a person.

The Pastor as a Choosing Person

This final chapter is the most personal of my reflections on the pastor as a person. The pastor as his or her choices is at the center of my psychology and my theology. Many years ago in seminary, my old mentor, T. A. Kantonen, once quoted someone as saying: "You cannot *ooze* into the kingdom of God; you *choose* in."[196] My later studies in philosophical and theological existentialism confirmed the centrality of choice for human freedom and responsibility. But Kantonen also reminded me of the words of Jesus: "You did not choose me, but I chose you" (John 15:16). My choices are best understood within the context of my having first been chosen.[197] That I have been chosen gives me not only greater responsibility but also greater freedom.

I have used my freedom to present the pastor as a person who has very human problems. Among those problems are the pastor's concern about overextension and how he or she is "seen" by others. The pastor also has very human difficulties with grief and loneliness and anger. I have not presented the pastor as knowing all the answers. On the contrary, I have suggested that the pastor may not even know all of the right questions.

I feel free to raise these kinds of issues because I have personally experienced all these concerns, and some of them still give me trouble. I know what it is like to feel trapped when I have been overwhelmed with work or beset by unreasonable demands and expectations, and to struggle to make sense of some personal loss while trying to function as a pastor to others in their grief, and to be locked into a conflict with a parishioner or a parish. At those times the last thing I thought I had was much choice.

In this chapter I want to share my personal perspective on some things a pastor may want to consider as he or she seeks to grow as a person and as a professional. Implicit in all that I say is my belief that the pastor's most powerful proclamation is made through his or her choices. But choosing takes courage. That courage comes from remembering that God has chosen us in Christ Jesus. Because we are chosen, we dare take the risks involved in choosing.

Choice as Risk

Pastors are not likely to lead the way in risk taking. I knew some risk takers in seminary, and I have known some as colleagues in ordained ministry, but not very many. People who really like to take risks are not going to be attracted in large numbers to a profession charged with conserving the heritage of the past, and this is true not only in the church but in any institution with strong traditions.

However, the pastor is chosen by God to *lead* God's people. While there is a place for leadership that has continuity with the past, the direction of God's call is not into the past but into God's future. The pastor has a priestly role, but also a prophetic role. The priestly function is a conserving function, but the prophetic is forthtelling and future-directed. The prophetic message is that the future is God's, and it is a choice. So the pastor is called to provide pastoral care, but also to call God's people to choose a faithful future. I believe it is true to the Bible to say that we choose a faithful future by accepting Christ as Savior and then each day choosing to live our faith. Faith has that paradoxical feel—forever, and one day at a time.

If faith is a choice forever and today, then pastors as persons need to become more attuned to risk taking. The reason is simple: there is no choice without risk. Pastor Joan realized that when she was asked to choose between staying at First Community or accept the call to St. James. She knew that when you say yes to one thing, you must inevitably say no to another.[198] The possible is possible only at a price of what presently exists. Joan could not go to St. James and stay at First Community. She could not both run from her problems and at the same time stand still and face them. The choice of one meant the loss of the other.

The choice for change not only involves the risk of losing something familiar or important to us. Our personal *identity* is always involved in what we think, feel, or do. I have suggested that our identity inheres in our wholeness as a bodily, thinking, feeling, relating, believing person—so much so that it is appropriate (although not adequate) to say: "I *am* my body," or "I *am* my feelings." As a whole person, we have a history and live in a situation which is our world. It is through our choices that we write the next page in our personal history. Any choice we make to change our life situation will change in some way our identity. As systems theory teaches us, a change in any part of the system changes the whole system. I think that applies to the individual as well as to a family or a congregation.

Sometimes it is less painful to stay the same.[199] Pastor Tom had come to know himself in his workaholic way. There is a certain security in that, even though it was killing him.[200] Pastor Joan was being suffocated by her role, but for her to choose to approach her role and herself differently meant that she had to face the strength of her sexuality and her fear. Pastor John could avoid the darkness of his own thoughts and feelings only if he insulated himself from the pain of others. Pastor Chris thought his security depended on riding the waves until retirement. Each of these pastors, in one way or another, was struggling for survival, as if life depended on things remaining the same.

In one respect, the life we have chosen for ourselves *does* depend on things remaining the same. Tom correctly intuits that truth, as do Joan and John and Chris. If Tom does something about his approach to work, his life will *not* be the same. He knows where he stands with the congregation as things are now. He does not know where things would stand if there were a change. But the new life to which we are called in Christ Jesus challenges us to give up our old securities and reliance on our own efforts to keep things under control. Christ calls us to take the risk of letting go so God can work his will in us.

Choosing Death

A biblical way to express this is that Christ calls us into death—death of the old person, the old ways, the life supports we have fashioned with our blood, sweat and tears—and sometimes the equally great sacrifices of those close to us. We have seen with all the pastoral situations we have discussed that change involves potential loss. We have also observed that underlying our fear of loss is our fear of death. Since the call to choose Christ each day is a call daily to die to self, we are called into what we most fear. No wonder most of us are willing to keep things as they are, even though our bodies or minds or hearts are crying for something new. When Kierkegaard said that to move *from* a spot you have to move *at* the spot, he knew full well the anxiety of a faith which calls a person into death.

I may be more willing than some to take the risk of choosing change; however, I confess to avoiding "death" as much as any of my pastoral colleagues. Even when I decide to take the risk of choosing change, I try to reduce the risk to me as a person. I try every way I know to change an uncomfortable situation before I even consider the need to change my way of being in the situation. I try to move *from* the spot without personally moving *at* the spot. I have tried such maneuvers with my own stress, my own role tensions, my grief, and my interpersonal conflicts. It doesn't work well for long.

Pastor Tom has a problem with workaholism, and so do I. I cannot choose to deal with my workaholism all at once. I can make that choice only one day at a time, and only I can make that choice—not my wife or my children or my colleagues or my students. There is a certain security, a kind of works righteousness, in demonstrating my worth through what I do. Christ calls me to the righteousness of faith, which is a call for me to choose the death of my self-sufficiency. I am continually impressed with the ways I manage to avoid this call into death. Each day is a new struggle. I do not understand my own behavior. What I want to do I don't do, and what I don't want to do I end up doing. I have the desire to keep my work activities in balance with the rest of my life and relationships, but it is really tough to keep my priorities straight.

The only times I have ever experienced my choices as leading to a new way is when I have chosen to risk following Christ into death. In the liturgical expression of my faith, this has meant saying, and meaning, that I am indeed sinful and centered in myself. In thought, word, and deed—not only by outward expression but also by secret thoughts and desires—I repeatedly turn away from my Lord and toward myself. My situation may be impossible, the demands for my time and presence may be inordinate, and others may contribute to its being as bad as it is, but my situation is not the cause of my problem. I am responsible for me. I cannot change anyone else. I cannot even change myself. But I can choose to allow myself to be changed by Christ.

The word for repentance, *metanoia*, means "turning around" or "changing my thinking." When I have turned around in my way of looking at myself in relation to a personal or pastoral problem, then, and only then, have I begun to move *at* the spot. I have learned that the risk of choice is always personal, or I am not really risking at all.

When the apostle Paul came to grips with his compulsions, his strength did not lie in his character or his willpower. Paul's hope was in the Christ who set Paul free. All Paul could say was "Thanks be to God" (Rom. 7:15—8:2). Because choice carries with it the risk of the death of the old, the pastor as a person needs a source of courage. Paul Tillich was perceptive when he called such courage "the courage to be."[201] He articulated courage as arising out of our acceptance of having been accepted. I think this is close to what I mean when I say that my courage to choose even "death" comes from my conviction that in Christ I have been chosen. Thanks be to God!

Choice as risk is, of course, only half the dynamic. The promise of God is that if we die with Christ we shall also rise with him. This is our eschatological hope, but resurrection is the promise in our daily "deaths" as well. One way to conceptualize this new life is to think of it as the challenge inherent in the choice to change.

Change as Challenge

One of my brothers once showed me that the Chinese picto-gram for *crisis* is the character for *danger* juxtaposed with the Chi-nese symbol for *opportunity*. Gerald Caplan defined a crisis in ex-actly this way—a danger and an opportunity.[202] Crisis interven-tion is oriented not only to supporting persons in threatening times, but also toward helping persons experience the opportuni-ty a crisis brings. The possibility is that the outcome of the critical situation may lead to personal integration at a level even higher than existed before the crisis began.

A crisis becomes a crisis because someone perceives a situa-tion as a significant threat. A crisis becomes a challenge when that person perceives the danger as an opportunity. What we choose to see is what makes change a challenge.[203]

When Pastor Tom was confronted by his physician, he pri-marily experienced a threat to his way of going about his life. Tom simply did not perceive that the physician's diagnosis was the first step toward healing and wholeness. Tom did not realize that God was speaking to him through the medical doctor, nor did he recognize that a physical crisis is necessarily a spiritual cri-sis.

Even with my (w)holistic orientation, I would probably have felt the same kind of threat Tom did—at least initially. Such an immediate negative reaction to the need for change is character-istic of those who are in ministry.[204] Maybe it is characteristic of people generally, and the pastor's awareness of being more like other people than different from them can help us be more sensi-tive to persons facing difficult transitions in their lives.

But the real challenge is what we do after the initial shock and emotional reaction. My personal experience illustrates the problem. When change is necessary, I often try to change no more than I absolutely have to. When I experienced burnout symptoms in the parish, I modified my schedule a little. That worked for a time, but soon I slipped back into the same old pat-terns. When I found myself, like Pastor Joan, trying to meet the unrealistic expectations of the pastoral role, and, worse, laying them on myself, I asserted myself—probably a little aggressively, as those who are nonassertive tend to do when they first try to be assertive. I let the church council know I was only human. Then I returned to my superhuman efforts to meet the needs which never seemed to end.

What I did not do was face the truth of myself—my limitations, my humanity, my mortality, my inability to change enough, in and of myself, apart from God's help. Like Pastor John I wanted a deathless resurrection, or like Pastor Chris I wanted a conflictless reconciliation. I wanted a change, but not enough to "die."

Choosing Life

The challenge of change is what emerges on the other side of our choice to die daily with Christ. It is the possibility that grows out of our recognition that all is not well and our decision to surrender self-will to our Savior.[205] It is what happens when we enter into our stressful situation, asking God to help us learn from it what he would have us know about ourselves—for our sake, and for the sake of our ministry to others.

The challenge of change is the opportunity that change provides for us to move toward wholeness as a person—as an individual, as a person in relationship with other persons, and in relationship with God. In my early studies with Elisabeth Kübler-Ross and the terminally ill, I was impressed with the way critical illness can affect a person's perception and values.[206] Illness can be like a Hezekiah's tunnel experience, where for Pastor Tom the whole world was reduced to the tunnel. One of the differences between the critically ill and the physically healthy is that the ill person seems to have a smaller world. My research demonstrated that, for the hospitalized, the world was often reduced to their hospital room, their bed, their body.[207] As Anton Boisen, Harry Stack Sullivan, the existentialists, and others have taught us, situations of extremity (like terminal illness and mental illness) can guide us to important truths of our life.[208] These truths are no less true during the good times. My body always has the potential to teach me something new about the world. My body can open me to a larger world as well as make it seem as though the world is getting smaller.

When my body starts giving out signals of distress, as Tom's did, I go to a physician. But I also take those signals as a possible sign that I have been letting my world get too small. I may be honing in too sharply on a part of my life at the expense of the whole. If the physician sees no organic basis for my complaint, then I wonder if God is using my body to speak a word I have failed to hear in any other way. Have I been trying to *include* too much (work, responsibility, physical activities that deny my age). But I also look to see if I have been *excluding* too much. Am I out of balance? Have I focused on intellectual tasks or emotional attachments to the point that there has been no room for physical exercise or wider social relationships or spiritual discipline?

Life can get out of balance not only by including or excluding too much. We can have neither too much nor too little of the right people and right things in our life, but still be unbalanced. A balanced life rightly discerns not only some sort of golden mean, but also where life's true treasures are to be found. In my research with the critically ill, I found that there was a statistically significant difference between what ill and healthy people felt to be most important.[209] The ill highly valued close, meaningful relationships. The healthy individuals expressed less need of others in their daily life. At times I have found that I take for granted the love and support of my wife and children, and do not nourish those relationships. My time is spent with other people and their needs, or with my own projects. There is nothing wrong with being available for others or doing important jobs. But it is possible that I have the right people and the right things, but in the wrong order.

I am not only a person, however, but also a person in relationships. For a pastor, the physical, mental, and emotional dimensions are much the same as they are for every other person, even though, broadly speaking, we have noted certain pastoral personality characteristics that may differentiate those who enter ordained ministry from those who enter some of the other professions. However, the pastor has a qualitatively different social dimension than other professionals, because of the way the ordained minister lives with those he or she serves. The social dimension for the pastor includes the laity.

Choosing Ministry

An unbalanced relationship between the pastor and the laity causes or contributes to many of the problems of pastoral ministry. The pastors in this book who had the most obvious problems with the clergy-lay balance were Tom, Joan, and Chris. Tom assumed the responsibility personally to do everything that needed to be done in the parish. Joan allowed herself to play a role that kept her from being a person among persons. Chris was reluctant to take the risk of losing his place at St. Peter's, and so his ministry was never authenticated as interdependent with the laity and mutually dependent on God.

Tom, Joan, and Chris share with me and perhaps many pastors the fear of that daily "death" to self without which we cannot rise to ministry. But one of the things that has to die with us is the way we ordained pastors usually define ministry. A "death" that has long needed to occur is the death of the pastor's notion that he or she is a minister and the rest of the congregation is the laity.[210] For the situation of Tom or Joan or Chris ever to be much different, they would have to perceive the challenge that comes from realizing that a pastor is simply a minister among ministers. Even a pastor's special call to preach the Word of God and administer the sacraments does not make him or her any more of a minister than any other Christian. The special functions of the ordained are not to set the pastor above any other person, but simply to help the pastor fulfill his or her particular calling to equip God's people for ministry.[211]

Most of the problems I have experienced with pastoral stress or role tensions have originated in my slowness to accept that I am only a minister among ministers. The harder I worked at being *the* minister in the congregation, accepting the role expectations of many and most importantly my own, the more imbalanced my ministry became. With the imbalance came my increased vulnerability to stress and to the frustration of having so much to do and feeling so alone in the doing of it. My efforts to change, as I said earlier, were unsuccessful because I wanted to change too little. I needed to die to the role I had assumed in order to rise to a shared ministry with my brothers and sisters in the congregation.

The heart of the matter is spiritual. The pastor is only a man or a woman. The more self-sufficient the pastor becomes, the less he or she needs God and the less Christ can be seen in that pastor's ministry. The witness of a superpastor's life is more clearly heard than any preaching done from the pulpit. The laity may feel dependent in congregations with such pastors, but they are more likely to be dependent on that pastor than on Christ. The members wonder what they would do without their pastor. When I hear this voiced as a serious concern in a congregation, and especially if I hear it directly or indirectly from the pastor, I have to wonder whether that pastor has helped God's people discover where their real security lies. I also wonder why the pastor might feel the need to hide behind such illusions of indispensability. Only God can give us the courage to let go of those pretensions that keep us from him and from each other.

The challenge of change, then, is the opportunity that change provides for us to grow toward wholeness as a person. When we are seeing ourselves in healthy perspective, our relationship to a ministry context is also more balanced and wholesome. When pastor and people are united in common dependence on God, the faithfulness of God is their strength, and the promise of Christ to be with them always is their assurance. Our Christian hope is built on nothing less.

Still, there are pastors in the position of Tom and Joan who are right in the midst of their personal and pastoral crises. You may be among them, as I have been. How can a pastor make the most of a crisis while it is being experienced? I believe one key to turning the lock that our present circumstances seem to have on us is to choose to see a critical time in our lives as *God's* time.

Crisis and *Kairos*

There are people who say they genuinely enjoy a crisis situation. Their personality is such that they find the danger stimulating, and they feel more alive and powerful when they master the critical event.

I have never enjoyed being in a personal crisis of my own. When a physician suspected a malignant tumor in my neck and under my arm and scheduled surgery as soon as possible, I felt that I was in a very dark place and that time was running out. And I felt like running. The physician may have enjoyed the challenge of the crisis, but I did not. When I was in the parish and my workload was buckling my knees and no relief was in sight, or when a conflict within the congregation yielded to no efforts to reconcile it and there seemed no place else to go, those felt like long tunnels with no light at the end.

Crisis in Space and Time

Being a human means being bound by space and time. That is why on the (w)holistic model I have emphasized both a person's situation (space) and a person's history (time). In saying "I am my history" and "I am my situations," a link is being established between personal time and space and my identity as a person.

If I reflect on how I have been in a crisis situation, I am aware that my perception of space and time is altered. I see differently. I feel things I do not usually feel. I act in less integrated ways. My sense of who I am is threatened. My experience is a lot like Tom's in Hezekiah's tunnel. The walls come in, the ceiling comes down, the water rises. Staying with the analogy, in the tunnel my vision is focused only on the next, tiny step that I hesitantly take, while my heart pounds for fear that it is a misstep. My usual ability to think my way through a situation is lost as my mind races nonproductively around the same track, which keeps getting smaller and more constricted. While I usually feel a broad range of complex emotions, in a crisis my feelings are much more likely to be variations on two feelings: anger (fight) and fear (flight). My sensitivity to the needs of others is lost as my interpersonal world along with the physical world collapses into the tunnel.

I have found that in the parish there are many Hezekiah's tunnels. Not only Tom, but also Joan and John and Chris all felt their space getting smaller and smaller, squeezing out the life they had come to know. When the pressure becomes too great, the expectations too high, the transitions too tough, the conflicts too intense, the tunnel seems long indeed. In situations of chronic pressure, frustration, or conflict, pastors, like all other people, tend not to think creatively. We fall back on the old, the tried, the familiar patterns that have worked in the past. Of course, one of the definitions of a crisis is that the old ways of coping no longer are adequate to the critical situation, and so the crisis deepens.[212]

The Valley of the Shadow

The psalmist expressed the existential crisis experiences of the people of God in the metaphor of "the valley of the shadow of death." When I was in Israel, I saw some of those craggy, rock-strewn, deeply shadowed valleys and I could only imagine what it would be like to go through one of them in the darkness, alone.

The biblical metaphor is especially helpful because it both captures the closing in feeling of a crisis and suggests a way to look at the altered sense of time.[213] In a crisis it is not just space that collapses; time does too. Time hangs heavy; it seems endless. As the darkness of the valley closes in, there is a desire to flee from the darkness, to run through the valley. The anxiety of a crisis reduces our life to a valley and propels us to rush through, just as fast as we possibly can.[214] We want out of the place where the darkness covers our hope, where no one seems to have the answers, and even God seems to be silent. We feel a tremendous press to get beyond the painful moment.

When Kierkegaard talked about moving *from* the spot, he was saying something similar to what I see in a crisis situation. People in the tough places of life want to move from the spot, and to do that fast. Tom wants relief from his physical symptoms; Joan wants a fuller, more satisfying life; John wants to go on as if nothing had happened; Chris wants things to be in order and under control. And they want those things *now*. But we have seen that real movement *from* a painful place requires a movement of the person *at* that critical spot.

Kairotic Time

If we integrate the Old Testament image of the valley and the New Testament conception of time, we are better able to perceive the potential for Christian pastors in a time of crisis. Up to now we have been talking about *chronological* time. "I am my history" has underlined the way my present is related to my past, and the past can be calendarized and chronicled. The Greek word for that kind of time is *chronos*. Time in the New Testament can be understood differently.[215] The Christ event has transformed *chronos* time into a qualitatively different kind of time called *kairos*. *Kairos* time is a time of God's inbreaking, his entering in a decisive way into the *chronos* of our lives. *Kairos* time is not controllable by us. We cannot create a *kairos*. It is a gift of grace. While we cannot cause a *kairos*, we can be *open* to a *kairos* when it comes.

My *kairos* times have come in the context of crisis, the dark valleys of my life. Whether a threat to physical life or professional identity or interpersonal relationship, I have never experienced a *kairos* while running from my problem. A *kairos* calls us to stay at the spot long enough to move. We must not run through the valley. It is understandable why most of the time we try to run. The danger is present and our instinct is to save our life. But to run through the valley is to reduce a potential *kairos* to a *chronos*, and apart from Christ any effort to save our life is really to lose it.

If the crises of the pastor as a person are to be the *kairotic* times they can become by God's grace, then we have to learn to do something other than follow our instincts. We have to follow our faith. Our instincts press us to run; our faith invites us to walk through the valley of the shadows of our lives.[216] God's supportive presence is the psalmist's hope as he walks through the valley of the shadow, even the shadow of death. The promise of the Word of God is not to those who run, but to those who walk in the faith that they do not walk alone. For a pastor to choose to walk when he or she feels like running is a risk, but I have personally found no way to be radically open to God while running and relying on my own resources. My growth as a pastor and as a person has involved my becoming vulnerable and choosing to find my strength not in myself but in Christ.

Tom is used to running, and it will not be easy for him to stop long enough to see the *kairotic* potential of his situation. The same is true for John and Chris. Joan appears to be closer to opening herself to change, beginning with her choice to acknowledge her own need in the course of responding to her distressed clergy colleague. For Joan, this confession was the beginning of a new life and ministry, a *kairos* gift of God.

While we have been considering crisis and *kairos* primarily in relation to pastoral situations, my work with the terminally ill taught me that there is something equally important to learn about *kairos* and a pastor's personal history. A person in a critical situation reexperiences (recapitulates) the life cycle conflicts. I want to share some additional personal history about this perception, and then apply it to *kairos* and history.

At the University of Chicago, my research with the critically ill was initiated when I was learning about the developmental theories of Erik Erikson. What I began to see with those in a life-threatening crisis was that the critically ill seemed to be struggling with their developmental conflicts all over again, especially the negative feelings of mistrust, shame, doubt, guilt, inferiority, isolation, stagnation, and despair; and with all of those feelings there was a pervasive sense of identity loss.[217] The person's whole world was changing and he no longer knew where he fit in. It seemed to me that, facing death, the terminally ill were recapitulating their whole life cycle in a final identity crisis, which I saw as a search for wholeness and, theologically, for salvation.[218]

Later, while working with a mental health center, I began to realize that not only terminal illness, but any serious stress or loss seemed to have the same effect. In a crisis a person struggles once more with all of those early and painful feelings. In other words, a crisis taps into experiences that we may or may not remember and compels us to do something with our past history as well as with our present situation.

In response to this challenge that a crisis seemed to create, I began at the mental health center a form of crisis intervention that I called the Kairos Group.[219] My goal was not to offer the persons in crisis a way to "fix" their situation, but a new way to perceive it. The persons' lives seemed to them to have fallen apart. Our group work was not to run from those feelings, but to enter into them and to help each person in the group put together the pieces in a new and more integrated way.

It was not appropriate in that context to explore the theological dimensions of the healing ministry that the Kairos Group involved, unless it was introduced by one of the group. Most of the time that did not occur. My choosing to leave the secular field and teach in the seminary was in part motivated by my need openly to witness to healing and wholeness as gifts of God in Christ Jesus.

That healing is not only of the present, but also of the past. Christians need not say the past is past and there is nothing we can do about it. During a time of crisis, God can give us the *kairotic* gift of reexperiencing the feelings that arose out of our most painful past memories, those experiences that may have led to our being less trustful, less open, less caring, less whole. If we are willing to walk, not run through those shadows and those feelings, Christ can lead us through the valley to choose a way of life that no longer reflects the scars of the past as much as it shines with the light of Christ. In this way, the past is the past, but when in a crisis portions of the past become present, there is a great deal that God enables us to do with it. When we are open to this healing of the past and the present, we are prepared in a new way to enter God's future.[220] That is *kairos*! In the giving of himself in Christ Jesus, God has made it known that he wills a *kairos*-life for each of us.

Tom brought a personal history to his stressful ministry situation, as did Joan and John and Chris. The crises each of them experienced were opportunities to resolve the problems of the present stress. But those crises were also challenges to let the Lord help them heal the parts of their past that kept them from seeing their worth apart from their works or their roles.

Ministry of Translucence

When a pastor chooses to run from the crises in life, the pastor's life is less than it might be and he or she may find ministry more difficult. Sensitivity to what is our own situation and time helps us to be more sensitive to those we serve. Pastoral care in a time of crisis or suffering is a faithful following of another person into the valley of the shadow, discerning that person's time, understanding the press from the environment and the individual's desire to run, but encouraging them by our presence to walk.[221]

The likelihood of a parishioner choosing to walk through such a dark place seems to me to be related only in part to our willingness to be present. The pastor is also called to be translucent to the light of Christ. If we pastors have not allowed Christ to lighten our personal darkness, it is hard for much light to be carried through us. Our own anxiety may propel us to fill the anxious spaces of the person in crisis with platitudes or premature assurances, with something that basically says that things are not so bad as they seem. Our own anxiety may cause us to be as impatient as the sufferer is with God's silence. Our own anxiety may contribute to our reluctance to wait on the Lord. And our own anxiety may heighten our desire to help the person seek his or her own salvation, a way out rather than into and through the crisis. Our personal need to provide an answer, perhaps our personal need to *have* an answer for ourselves, may cause us to intrude into the questioning space of the parishioner. The parishioner, of course, wants to make the situation safer and will seem to welcome our anxious efforts. But, distressful as it is, this time and this space is a potential *kairos* gift of God. Persons in crisis need a pastor who is willing to support them, and, when it is time, to assist them in raising the real, deep questions of life that arise out of the critical experience. Persons in crisis need pastors able to help them remain open to *kairos*.

Kairos time, as we have said, is not our time. It is God's time; it is grace-full time. In faith that we have the Answer to share, pastors dare resist the temptation to provide answers. When we are moving through the constricting, scary, dark places and spaces in our life, it is important to recall the most valuable lesson that came out of Pastor Tom's experience in Hezekiah's tunnel. Remember, when things were the darkest and all hope seemed to be lost, suddenly Tom realized that he was not alone. Contrary to any reasonable expectation, a little boy appeared from the other side of the tunnel. So, too, in the pastor's personal Hezekiah's tunnels of life and as he or she offers a translucent presence to other persons stumbling in the dark shadows of their despair, we are reminded of One who came as a child, from the other side— One who continues to meet us at those most helpless and hopeless times, One whose life and death and resurrection penetrate our darkness with the light of his promise, "There is a way!," One who leads us through the closed-in tunnels of our lives to an open place, where there is healing and wholeness.[222]

Christ and Commitment

The way of Christ is the way of commitment. When I was growing up, I understood this to mean that if I wanted to be a Christian then I must be willing to be a committed Christian. Committed meant good. In other words, it was all up to me. As I sowed, so would I reap. Sowing meant doing the right things, the Christian things; reaping meant God's approval and, even more important, God's acceptance.

I believe those who taught me this understanding of commitment were well-intentioned Christians. Unfortunately, they somehow had missed the gospel. Perhaps that is why I saw such intensity in their faces and their activities. There was little time for a more relaxed approach to life. Their faith was work, and they worked hard. I learned to do the same. I may have been doing the right things, but I was doing them for the wrong reason.[223] I was looking at Christian commitment as though my life depended on it. For someone like me who did not always measure up to the biblical standards, this way of looking at commitment was not good news at all.

Rightly understood, the gospel is good news indeed. In Christ Jesus, God has shown unconditional love toward us, a commitment so complete that it took the shape of a cross.[224] As symbolized by the cross, God's grace extends to the height and depth and length and breadth of our lives. God's commitment in Christ is forever—and for today.

Since God gives us grace day by day, our response is with our whole life, day by day. The way we choose to live the days of our lives is our way of saying thanks to God. Christian commitment is therefore not a way to be assured of salvation. Commitment as a Christian is on the resurrection side of the cross. It is a free choice made by those who have already been chosen in Christ.

I have stressed the nature of commitment as beginning with God's choice because I want the specific illustrations and suggestions that follow to be understood as free and happy responses to God's love, no better and no more faithful than the sincere responses made by others. My observations have nothing to do with anyone's acceptability to God. Acceptance depends on God's choice of us, not our choice of the right way to come to God.

Personal Responses to Grace

Once I accept my freedom in the gospel, I am able to consider the many ways in which I can choose to be strengthened as a person and as a pastor. Over the years I have found that some things work for me, and some do not. Most of my adult life I did a little physical exercise here and a little reading or meditation there, and my work load usually squeezed out whatever I did before very long. In most recent years, I have taken seriously the implications of my (w)holistic model, and I have done what is the most difficult thing for many teachers. What I have taught others, I have tried to apply to myself.

I have found it useful and sometimes even necessary to place my model before me and ask whether my approach to self-care and ministry is as a partial person or as a whole person. What I want to share with you now is the shape of my response to God for his gift of life and his call to ministry. My response reflects my personality, my history, and my ministry situation. There may be some things that transfer reasonably well to your ministry and some things that would not fit either you or your situation. If nothing else, perhaps the (w)holistic thought and feeling behind my chosen response will be of some value as you consider the shape of your own commitment. As an overview, my notes on my personal commitment look like this:

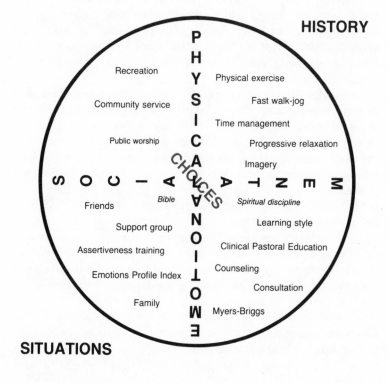

There is considerable literature on the value of a number of my notes to myself, for example, in the areas of nutrition, meditation, and physical exercise.[225] I want to comment only on my commitments that represent an opportunity that might not be readily apparent. Physically, I have found that the stress of everyday life produces in me more muscle tension that I once realized. Psychologist friends of mine about seven years ago invested in biofeedback equipment for their office and invited me as a colleague to try it out.[226] Biofeedback enables a person to measure such things as body temperature, muscular tension, and skin conductivity. Attached by wires to the machine, I listened to the beeps and tones that signaled more or less relaxation. I thought I felt relaxed, but the machine said I was tense.

What really convinced me was when my colleagues asked me to perform a mental task with numbers. I concentrated on the task. The tones raised, and the beeps were more insistent. That meant increased tension. However, I did well on the task. After several sessions with my friends, I learned to relax myself with thoughts and images, with the machine reinforcing me with more pleasant sounds.

One day my friends asked me to repeat the mental task, this time not concentrating, but relaxing. That was hard for me, but I did it. My performance was 150% of my earlier score. I could not believe it! Those results challenged what I thought I knew about myself. I had always thought that the answer to not doing well or enough was to try harder. When I reflected on that experience, I realized that perhaps doing better or more required that I in a sense do less. Maybe I would have more to offer others if I would relax and take a little time for myself. I chose to try this new approach. Before long, persons receiving my ministry commented on how much easier it was to talk with me when it did not seem as if they were keeping me from something else. Nouwen talks about creative ministry as "intangible tensions between self-affirmation and self-denial, self-fulfillment and self-emptying, self-realization and self-sacrifice."[227] I agree with Nouwen that Christian maturity moves increasingly in the direction of self-giving, but I believe the giving can be even greater when we have more to give. The stewardship of our bodies is a way to say thanks to God.

Biofeedback equipment can be portable, but I am not one who likes to be dependent on machines. A physician who used hypnosis in his medical practice told me about progressive relaxation exercises that he found helpful for his patients. I learned a form of the Jacobsen technique, which alternates brief periods of tension with longer periods of relaxation, starting at one point in the body and progressing to all other major points.[228] The adaptation I discovered to be most helpful for me started with the top of my head, proceeded down my face, neck and shoulders to both arms and hands, where I imagined the tension to be flowing out my fingers. Then with a deep breath I began alternating tension and relaxation in my chest, back, abdomen, legs, and feet, with the remaining tension flowing out my toes. There are many variations of relaxation, but this worked best for me if I spent about 15 minutes a day doing it. I found nighttime best, and sometimes drifted off to sleep before I was completely finished.

After a while I became bored with the relaxation routine, but still impressed with the benefits for my body and my work. Years ago, Paul Tournier suggested that the physical offers an especially good opportunity for spiritual integration.[229] I decided to approach my relaxation in ten steps, each step associated with a different part of my body and matched with a portion of the Lord's Prayer. The result is something like this: as I relax my head and face, I think about what it means to have God our Father at the head of all creation. With God in control, I can dare let go. I pray for his presence with me as I attempt to relax myself so as better to be able to serve. Since I speak God's name with my larynx, I relaxed my neck and shoulder area as I prayed: "Hallowed be thy name," and, with Luther, I ask that his name be holy for me. The psalmist's proclamation that "God's holy arm has won him the victory" comes to my mind as I relax my arms with "Thy kingdom come." The image of the healing, helping hands of Jesus enable me to relax my own with "Thy will be done. . . ." With a deep breath (the breath of life) and a slow exhalation that expands and relaxes my chest all the way down to my stomach, I pray, "Give us this day our daily bread." Sin being something on my back, so to speak, and something I would like to be behind me, reminds me to relax my back as I pray, "And forgive us our trespasses as we forgive those who trespass against us." "Lead us not into temptation" focuses my attention on my abdomen, starting with my stomach and progressing down, and the strong image of the children of God using their legs to leave Egypt during the Exodus and later walking back to Jerusalem after their captivity in Babylon helps me concentrate on my legs and God's deliverance from evil. Standing on the solid rock of Christ is a helpful image for focusing on my feet and the kingdom of God. The rest of the doxology I breathe with a prayer that as the remaining tension flows out my toes I will be free to show forth God's power and glory without letting my own tensions and anxieties get in the way.

I have been integrating various scripture passages, Christian creeds, prayer, and relaxation in this and similar ways for about six years, and I have found it an effective way for me to relax while remembering who I am and whose I am. There are some cautions Christians need to observe in attempting an integration like this. Most importantly, the Lord's Prayer has an integrity of its own. It is not directed toward personal ends, but toward God's higher purposes. I continue to remind myself not to *use* the Lord's Prayer, but to allow our Lord's Prayer to help me speak to God and let God use me in ministry. A more relaxed body and open approach to persons can be one way to follow Paul in his desire to "pray without ceasing." When I get too busy even to take the time to pray the Lord's Prayer and relax my tensions, then I know that I have allowed my life once more to get badly out of balance. That is a sign that I need to let go of my efforts to accomplish all things myself, and let God help me regain my perspective—and my humility.

While physical relaxation has mental and emotional benefits, as well as spiritual implications, there are other valuable approaches to self-care. I have found no good substitute for a formal or informal counseling (or consultation) relationship with a professional colleague or trusted friend. The Clinical Pastoral Education movement, while not intended to be a substitute for personal counseling, does provide a context where many come to a keener self-understanding. It is possible for a pastor who has never received counseling to counsel a parishioner, but I cannot imagine how it could be as sensitive or effective. Acknowledging my own need and my dependence on others and on God helps me to see the needy persons I counsel as brothers and sisters, and having been in dark valleys of my own helps me know when to speak and when to keep silence with them.

Personal Gifts

Another way I have become aware of how my personality affects my ministry is through instruments like the Myers-Briggs Type Indicator.[230] I became familiar with the MBTI in the mid-1970s when I was at the mental health center in Florida. During the past several years I have become increasingly interested in how the MBTI can be useful for persons who want to understand not only themselves but also the way they can best minister to others.[231] The Myers-Briggs is based on the theories of Carl Jung, a Swiss psychiatrist and the son of an Evangelical pastor. The test consists of 126 sets of words and phrases, and the test taker marks down which words or phrases are preferred. The result is a "type profile" which helps persons see how they typically perceive the world, how they make judgments or decisions about what is perceived, whether persons are drawn toward the outer world or pulled to a more private inner world, and the attitude with which one approaches the world, for example, how comfortable a person is with order and closure as compared with flexibility and open-endedness. Each "type" is presented as a "gift." [232] An increasing number of seminaries are using the MBTI to help students identify how their seminary years can best be used to consolidate their strengths and to improve areas of lesser strength.

In reviewing my MBTI profile, I learned that the Lord might be able to use my gift more fully if I did not indulge my preference for privacy quite so much. Unless I am willing to share my reflections, others never are given the opportunity to decide whether or not they might benefit from applying some of my perceptions. This book represents my effort to be more responsible with my inner thoughts. The MBTI also alerted me to the dangers of waiting until all the data is in before coming to a conclusion or a decision. I have been challenged to take more risks and leave the last word to God.

Perhaps the most sobering and helpful awareness was that, though I have many particular characteristics common to pastors, my overall profile is not frequently found. What an important thing for me to learn as I seek to be a better teacher to pastors! Not only did I realize the special contributions I could make in the seminary, but I also began to evaluate my teaching methods to be certain that they met more than my personal needs.

Gifts in Ministry

In the same way the MBTI opened me to a new way of conceptualizing my role in the classroom, so the MBTI opens the pastor to a number of additional perspectives on ministry. Ministry is to persons, and each of the parishioners may need a different kind of ministry, since there are a variety of ways a parishioner can perceive himself or herself and the world. Some of the conflicts that arise in the parish develop because people misperceive somebody's different way of seeing the world as being a deliberate affront to them. For example, on the MBTI a "sensing and thinking type" just naturally thinks of practicalities like money and time. An "intuitive feeling type" just naturally thinks of ideal possibilities for people. The two are likely to express very different sounding values in a church meeting planning for the future direction of ministry for a congregation in a deteriorating neighborhood. An appreciation for the gifts that *each* type has to offer the Christian community can help the pastor creatively *use* the differences. A knowledge of one's own and others' individual differences can also help the pastor know how best to help parishioners reconcile their differences when those differences have led each to be insensitive and depreciating of the contribution of the other.

Of course, not only pastors but also parishioners have a ministry. When we think about the ministry of the laity, we too often lump all laity together. The MBTI helps a pastor not only know his or her gifts, but the special gifts and ministries of others. It may well be that a lay person with certain gifts will better be able to minister to another member of the congregation than the pastor.

In addition to helping the pastor equip the laity for ministry, the MBTI may be of value in planning worship experiences. It appears that preferred forms of spirituality are related to differences that can be identified with the MBTI.[233] A person may be no less faithful when she chooses not to attend a mid-week service. It may simply be that the individual's spiritual growth does not lie in the direction of more services, but in another form of spirituality. The pastor who begins to appreciate the way differences among parishioners lead to differing spiritual expressions is likely to find a greater and grateful response to his or her efforts to provide alternative forms of spiritual direction and support. While no psychological instrument is the answer, pastors seeking to be more effective ministers can benefit from what God can teach us through a self-awareness and growth instrument like the Myers-Briggs.

Making Our Past a Gift

My use of the MBTI has helped me with many of the dimensions of a (w)holistic approach to myself and my ministry, but something beyond the Myers-Briggs is needed to help with our integration of our past into our present situation. Seminarians often bring to their studies some heavy burden from early life experiences within the family and sometimes within the church.[234] In pastoral care and counseling courses, it becomes clear that the experiences and assumptions that the student has affects the kind of response he or she is likely to give a person in need. Since so little time is spent in seminary with the healing of hurtful memories of the past, it is probable that most of a seminarian's "unfinished business" is taken into the parish. I continue to work with a Kairos Group in the seminary. This voluntary group shares life stories and situations. We strengthen our sense of being gifted by Christ with the capacity to choose a more fulfilling and personally freeing future. I have also found some forms of journaling to be helpful. While I have not been trained in the method, my colleagues have suggested the potential of the Progoff technique. Ira Progoff's journaling aims to help persons achieve harmony within themselves, with those around them (past and present), and with their life situation.[235] It is a system of dialog that helps a person identify and work through "unfinished business" from the past and be more fully and freely available for ministry in the present. While the seminary must pay more attention to the personal history and need for healing in the seminarian, perhaps those pastors who are already serving may find the Progoff methods helpful.

Now that I have shared with you some of the ways in which I have been helped better to express my commitment to Christ, I want to repeat the counsel with which this discussion began.

None of the techniques or methods I have discussed makes any lasting sense unless it is seen in relationship to the spiritual. None of them is a way to God, nor is one a better Christian for using them. They are tools. You may have methods that are more helpful for you and your ministry. What we Christians share in common is not our *way* of being thankful, but our *reason* for being thankful—God's gift of grace in Jesus Christ.

Spiritual Gifts

This leads me to say a parting word about the pastor's personal spiritual life. There is no one way to worship and no one way to spiritual discipline. It should be expected that persons will find significantly different ways to express commitment to God, none of which is necessarily more or less spiritual than the other.

In the seminary, spiritual formation is a continuing commitment and a current concern. I wonder whether many professors realize that we tend to try to shape a prospective pastor's personal devotional life and public worship practices according to the values of the faculty, rather than be guided by the spiritual needs of the individual student. A seminarian may comply while in school, but I have seen few pastors continue the seminary model after they are in the parish. I believe a more helpful approach would be to guide a student to discover that spiritual discipline contributes to the completion and integration of his or her personal and communal life. The (w)holistic model is a reminder that spirituality is not a part of life; it is integral to the daily living out of our faith. It may be expressed in the ordinary as well as the extraordinary. Since God's love is new every morning and worship is a response to that love, each day a person may need to consider a different form of spiritual expression. At certain times in our lives, or in particular vocational circumstances, those forms might vary even more. Rather than ask all seminarians to do the same thing as an expression of piety, students need to be helped to experiment with approaches to spirituality that will help them along their personal path to wholeness.

When a pastor has been trained to see spiritual discipline in this more flexible way, that pastor's daily devotions reflect his or her personal spiritual growing edges (always, of course, in responsible relationship to the whole body of Christ, for spiritual wholeness is relational). Some seminarians and some pastors need to learn (or relearn) the lessons of silence and solitude at a particular point in their life. Others may need to find some colleagues for a more corporate expression of faith, whether or not it is liturgical in form. Pastors who do not stop very often may find a time set aside for thinking or writing about the theological implications of a real life situation to be a devotional experience—as well as personally or pastorally helpful. Those who are inclined to turn inward may find spending a prescribed period each week in social ministry activities to be a faith-stretching way to worship God, for the Bible affirms those who complete their doing of devotions with the doing of justice. Spiritual formation is not the conforming to some mythical norm, but the personal discovery and celebration of our wholeness before God in whatever ways lead to and give expression to that wholeness.

I have found that reading and reflecting on Scripture is an important part of my day. Commentaries and other study aids help me to challenge my individual interpretations and maintain continuity with the historical witness of the church. Gathering on the Lord's Day with other Christians to share the Word and sacraments is another needed balance to my more private nature. Whatever shape it takes, I agree with Matthew Fox that "the fruits of a deeply spiritual life are always a wholistic personality."[236] I would go even further to suggest that the fruits of a deeply (w)holistic life are always a mature and sensitive spirituality.

Christian Choices

Finally, I want to comment on commitment and choices. I think it is important to point out that *what* we choose, as Christians, may have much less to do with faithfulness than the *way* we make those choices. When I apply the saying, "I am my choices," to Christian commitment, I am not suggesting that some choices are clearly Christian and others are not. As we have already indicated, persons can make the right choices for reasons that have little to do with Christ. I also believe that people may make what appear to be wrong choices while being very much concerned to be faithful to Christ. No one can see into the heart of a person, except God. How we come to make a choice has as much, or more, to do with commitment to Christ than the specific choice we make. Especially in some of the more difficult ethical decisions Christians are called to make in our time, we need to remember that God knows our hearts. God sees in our way of going about making choices our desire to be faithful. Nothing, not even the actual choice we make, can separate us from that love we have received in Jesus Christ.

I am a choosing person. I value having choices to make and my ability to make them. I have choices to make because I am free. The freedom is relative, and the available options are always limited. Yet, deep in my heart I know I am not totally bound by my personal history or my life situation. When God calls me to "choose life," the gift of freedom and choice come with the call. I thank God for these gifts.

But choices also scare me at times. To be free to choose means I am responsible for my choices. In this book I have chosen to present the pastor as a person. I have taken the risk of focusing on the human side of ministry. I am mindful that some people do not read a book through to the end. Such a reading of *Pastor as Person* may provide only an awareness of my strong emphasis on the pastor as a *person*. At the center of my concern *is* the pastor as a person, but I understand personhood to mean a person *in Christ*. To stop with the humanistic emphases I make leads to an unhealthy and an unfaithful orientation to self. The value of a (w)holistic model is that it reminds us of what happens when the self is emphasized apart from the world, or when the human is seen apart from the divine.

It is my hope that your reading of this book, as a seminarian preparing for the ordained ministry or as a pastor in the midst of ministry, has resulted in your feeling less alone in your struggles and more affirmed as a person. You matter—to God, to those whom you serve, and to your colleagues in ministry. Taking your wholeness as a gift of God, I challenge you to risk the changes that will open you to the *kairotic* inbreaking of Christ. You are a person with choices. I hope what I have shared will be of help as you choose life, today and each day, in the confidence that you yourself have already been chosen by God.

Notes

Preface

1. Throughout the book, I have tried to use inclusive language when referring to the pastor. Biblical masculine references to God and Jesus have been retained.
2. I was introduced to this experiential method by Charles R. Stinnette at the University of Chicago. Cf. C. R. Stinnette, "Existence and Faith: A Theological Method As Focused in Psycho-social Perspectives," Academy of Religion, Dallas, October 18, 1968. Stinnette acknowledges his indebtedness to such thinkers as Augustine, Dilthey, Scheler, Schelling, Merleau-Ponty, Ricoeur, and Erikson.

Chapter 1. The Pastor as Person: A (W)holistic Model

3. Oscar Cullmann, "Immortality or Resurrection," in Krister Stendahl, ed., *Immortality and Resurrection* (New York: Macmillan, 1965), pp. 9-53.
4. In this discussion and that which follows, I have been helped especially by Frank H. Seilhamer, *Here Am I: A Study of the Presence of God in the Old Testament and in the Writings of Luther* (Lima, Ohio: C.S.S. Publishing Co., 1972), pp. 23ff.; Ralph Doermann, "Life and Death in the Old Testament and Intertestamental Periods," unpublished paper based on the writings of Charles, Koehler, Johnson, Pedersen, von Rad, Robinson, Rowley, Russell, and Snaith; T. A. Kantonen, *Life After Death* (Philadelphia: Fortress Press, 1962), pp. 6-10; Gregory Baum, "Man in History: The Anthropology of Vatican II," in *The New Morality*, William Dunphy, ed. (New York:

Herder and Herder, 1967), pp. 157-173; Ben Johnson, "Biblical Perspective on Death and Dying," Convocation on Death, Dying, and Other Losses, Hamma School of Theology, 1978; and Hans Schwarz, *Beyond the Gates of Death* (Minneapolis: Augsburg Publishing House, 1981), pp. 17-36.

5. Kantonen, p. 9.
6. J. A. T. Robinson, quoted in Kantonen, p. 8. Cf. Seilhamer, p. 23.
7. Doermann and Kantonen, pp. 7ff., and Seilhamer, p. 27. Cf. James M. Childs Jr., *Christian Anthropology and Ethics* (Philadelphia: Fortress Press, 1978), pp. 50-66; Bernhard W. Anderson, *Understanding the Old Testament*, 3rd ed. (Englewood Cliffs, N.J.: Prentice-Hall, 1976), pp. 212, 289, 305, 356.
8. This is a notable theme in Martin Buber, *I and Thou*, trans. Walter Kaufmann (New York: Charles Scribner's Sons, 1970) and Paul Tillich, *Systematic Theology*, vols. 1-3 (Chicago: University of Chicago Press, 1951-63).
9. Doermann and Kantonen, pp. 7ff.
10. Variations of this model have proved helpful in my work with the terminally ill: "The Voice of the Dying," 1968, which will appear as "Death and Identity: Implications for Pastoral Care," in Brian O'Conner, ed., *Ministry and Thanatology* (New York: Archives of the Foundation of Thanatology); "Death: A Theological Reformulation of Developmental and Existential Perspectives" (University of Chicago, doctoral dissertation under Peter Homans, Elisabeth Kübler-Ross, and Joseph Sittler); workshops for the Ohio Funeral Directors Association and funeral directors in Florida and Illinois (1975-80) and various other pastors' groups; "Pace Study" research on stress in the seminary, 1980-83, reported in "Pace in Learning and Life: Prelude to Pastoral Burnout," in *Seminary and Congregation: Integrating Learning, Ministry, and Mission* (Association of Professional Education for Ministry, LeRoy H. Aden, ed.); "Pastoral Burnout: A View from the Seminary," with Evan Rogers, Statistician, in *Journal of Pastoral Care*, vol. 38, no. 2, June, 1984; "The Person in Ministry," *The Trinity Review* (Spring 1983), and in "The Person in Ministry: Psychological Type and the Seminary," *Research in Psychological Type* (Mississippi State University, 1984). The categories are those of the American Medical Association, and I was encouraged to think (w)holistically by the work of Paul Tournier and Granger E. Westberg. Cf. *The Healing of Persons*, written in 1940 (New York: Harper & Row, 1965), and *The Whole Person in a Broken World*, trans. J. and H. Doberstein (New York: Harper & Row, 1964), pp. 53ff., as well as *Minister and Doctor Meet* (New York: Harper & Row, 1961), pp. 52ff.
11. Cf. the principle of linkage in Daniel Day Williams, *The Minister and the Care of Souls* (New York: Harper & Row, 1961), pp. 26-27, and Wayne Oates' discussion of Williams in *The Christian Pastor*, 3rd rev. ed. (Philadelphia: Westminster Press, 1982), pp. 20ff.

12. Most importantly, Erik H. Erikson, *Childhood and Society*, 2nd ed. (New York: Norton, 1950, 1963), p. 261.
13. Willard D. Allbeck, who was trained in psychology and became a church historian, helped me to appreciate the historical perspective. The developmental theories of Freud and Erikson, interpreted by David L. Ostergren and Charles W. Stinnette, were my introduction to the person as history. Cf. Charles R. Stinnette, "Reflection and Transformation: Knowing and Change in Psychotherapy and in Religious Faith," relative to history, in Peter Homans, ed., *The Dialogue Between Theology and Psychology* (Chicago: University of Chicago Press, 1968), pp. 83ff. Cf. Paul Tournier, *The Seasons of Life* (Richmond: John Knox Press, 1963), trans. John F. Gilmour, p. 18.
14. I recommend the overview of developmental psychology in April O'Connell and Vincent O'Connell, *Choice and Change*, rev. ed. (Englewood Cliffs, N.J.: Prentice-Hall, 1980), pp. 17ff. The O'Connells' work is generally compatible with my (w)holistic concerns.
15. Jean Piaget and Barbara Inhelder, *The Psychology of the Child*, trans. Helen Weaver (New York: Basic Books, 1969).
16. Lawrence Kohlberg, *The Philosophy of Moral Development* (San Francisco: Harper & Row, 1981); James Fowler, *Stages of Faith: The Psychology of Development and the Quest for Meaning* (San Francisco: Harper & Row, 1981).
17. Daniel J. Levinson, et al., *The Seasons of a Man's Life* (New York: Alfred A. Knopf, 1978); Gail Sheehy, *Passages* (New York: Bantam, 1976).
18. Bernice Levin Neugarten, ed., *Middle Age and Aging: A Reader in Social Psychology* (Chicago: University of Chicago Press, 1968); for early and very recent work on pastoral issues, cf. Henri J. Nouwen, with Peter J. Naus and Don McNeill, "Aging and Ministry," *Journal of Pastoral Care* 28(3) (September 1974):164ff., and Arthur H. Becker's forthcoming book on pastoral ministry, *The Compassionate Visitor*, to be published by Augsburg Publishing House.
19. The discussion that follows is heavily dependent on Erik H. Erikson, *Childhood and Society* (New York: W.W. Norton & Co., Inc., 1950, 1963); "Growth and Crises of the Healthy Personality," *Psychological Issues* (New York: International University Press, 1959); *Identity: Youth and Crisis* (New York: Norton, 1968); *Young Man Luther* (New York: Norton, 1958). Cf. Richard I. Evans, *Dialogue with Erik Erikson* (New York: Harper & Row, 1967).
20. Carroll A. Wise, *The Meaning of Pastoral Care* (New York: Harper, 1966), pp. 88-117; Don S. Browning, *Generative Man: Psychoanalytic Perspectives* (Philadelphia: Westminster Press, 1973); and especially the works of Donald Capps, *Pastoral Care: A Thematic Approach* (Philadelphia: Westminster Press, 1979), pp. 25ff., and Capps' most recent work, *The Life Cycle and Pastoral Care* (Philadelphia: Fortress Press, 1983).

21. In addition to Erikson's works, cf. Salvatore R. Maddi, *Personality Theories*, 3rd ed., (Homewood, Ill.: Dorsey Press, 1976), pp. 292ff.; O'Connell and O'Connell, *Choice and Change*; David Rappaport, "A Historical Survey of Psychoanalytic Ego Psychology," in Erik Erikson, "Identity and the Life Cycle," *Psychological Issues* 1(1)(1959).

22. Cf. Bernhard W. Anderson, pp. 2ff.

23. Robert W. White, "Competence and the Psychosexual Stages of Development," in M. R. Jones, ed., *Nebraska Symposium on Motivation* (Lincoln, Neb.: University of Nebraska Press, 1960) and D. W. Fiske and S. R. Maddi, eds., *Functions of Varied Experience* (Homewood, Ill.: Dorsey Press, 1961).

24. Talcott Parsons, "Social Structure and the Development of Personality: Freud's Contribution to the Integration of Psychology and Sociology," in *Social Structure and Personality* (London: Free Press, 1964), pp. 78ff.

25. Cf. Browning, esp. pp. 9, 12, and 162ff.

26. The Midwest Career Development Service (Columbus, Ohio, Chicago, and Westchester, Ill.) attempts to assess nurturance and succorance during their vocational assessments (Frank C. Williams, D.Min., director, personal communication, Columbus).

27. Harbaugh, "Death: A Theological Reformulation of Developmental and Existential Perspectives." On the integrity and mission of the old, cf. Paul Tournier, *Learn to Grow Old* (New York: Harper & Row, 1972), pp. 42ff., 178ff., 209ff.

28. This insight of Anton T. Boisen is a key concept of clinical pastoral education. Cf. Charles Stewart with Maurice Clark, Len Cedarleaf, Al Meiburg, Bob Leslie, Don Worthy, Bill Oglesby, and Helen Terkelsen, "Living Issues in CPE: A Dialogue," *Journal of Pastoral Care* 29(3) (September 1975):148.

29. Tillich, *Systematic Theology*; Cf. Harry Stack Sullivan, *The Interpersonal Theory of Psychiatry*, Helen Swick Perry and Mary Ladd Gawel, eds. (New York: Norton, 1953), and Wayne E. Oates, *Pastoral Counseling* (Philadelphia: Westminster, 1974), pp. 65ff.

30. At the University of Chicago, I was sensitized to "the situation" by Peter Homans and especially by Eugene Gendlin in his course on existential psychotherapy. Cf. Gendlin, *Experiencing and the Creation of Meaning* (New York: The Free Press of Glencoe, 1962) and "Focusing," in *Psychotherapy: Theory, Research and Practice* 6(1) (Winter 1969). Gendlin valued the work of Jean-Paul Sartre and used as a text Sartre's *Being and Nothingness* (New York: Washington Square Press, 1953, 1969); Cf. Leland Elhard, "The Implications of Existentialism for Pastoral Theology," in William B. Oglesby Jr., ed., *The New Shape of Pastoral Theology: Essays in Honor of Seward Hiltner* (Nashville: Abingdon, 1969), pp. 139f. and Rollo May, "Contributions of Existential Psychotherapy," in *Existence: A New Dimension*

in Psychiatry and Psychology, R. May, E. Angel, and H. F. Ellenberger, eds. (New York: Basic Books, 1958).
31. Cf. Peter A. Homans, *Theology After Freud* (New York: Bobbs-Merrill, 1970), pp. 107ff.; Samuel H. Miller, "Pastoral Experience and Theological Training: The Implications of Depth Psychology for Christian Theology"; and Seward Hiltner, "Pastoral Counseling and the Ministry," in Hans Hofmann, ed., *Making the Ministry Relevant* (New York: Charles Scribner's Sons, 1960). See also Thomas W. Klink, *Depth Perspectives in Pastoral Work* (Philadelphia: Fortress Press, 1965) and Carl R. Rogers, *On Becoming A Person* (Boston: Houghton Mifflin, 1961). Seward Hiltner sensitized the theological community to the significance of Rogers' work for pastoral counseling in *Pastoral Counseling* (New York: Abingdon-Cokesbury, 1949). See also Don S. Browning, *Atonement and Psychotherapy* (Philadelphia: Westminster, 1966), pp. 94ff.
32. My initial introduction to systems theory was through seminars with Carl Whitaker. Cf. Gerald P. Erickson and Terrence P. Hogan, eds., *Family Therapy: An Introduction to Theory and Technique* (New York: Jason Aronson, 1976). In addition, helpful perspectives are provided by Jay Haley, Virginia Satir, Paul Watzlawick, Salvatore Minuchin, Peggy Papp, Ronald Fox, Marianne Riche, and Steve Jones of the Menninger Foundation.
33. The late Carl Nighswonger, chaplain colleague of Elisabeth Kübler-Ross, was especially interested in the God-questions implicit in experience, an interest evident in Nighswonger's religious restatement of the themes of Elisabeth Kübler-Ross, *On Death and Dying* (New York: Macmillan, 1969). Cf. Nighswonger, "Death and Dying," Care Cassettes, The American Protestant Hospital Association Series, College of Chaplains, Chicago, 1974, and the way John B. Cobb relates spirit and wholeness in *Theology and Pastoral Care* (Philadelphia; Fortress, 1977).
34. Søren Kierkegaard, T. A. Kantonen, Paul Tournier, Paul Tillich, Eugene Gendlin, Elisabeth Kübler-Ross, and Salvatore Maddi have contributed in different ways to my understanding of the person as his or her choices. Cf. Tournier, *The Meaning of Persons* (New York: Harper & Row, 1957), pp. 127ff., 198ff., *The Seasons of Life*, *The Adventure of Living* (New York: Harper & Row, 1965), *A Doctor's Casebook in Light of the Bible* (New York: Harper and Brothers, 1954, 1960); and an interesting summary and application by Paul E. Morrisette, "Jean-Paul Sartre and Rollo May: Their Relatedness and Their Contributions to Counseling," in *AMHC Forum* 28(2)(1975). No one has been more forceful in emphasizing choice than Kantonen, the eminent Lutheran theologian. About Luther, Kantonen once remarked: "Luther is, after all, basically an existentialist. Personal responsibility and choice are not peripheral issues, but central to Lutheran theology" (personal communication).

For additional references, see Harbaugh, "A Model for Caring," *Thanatos* (Winter 1983):24.

35. Joseph Sittler, course notes from "Theological Method and the Ecological Crisis," The University of Chicago, 1970, and *The Ecology of Faith* (Philadelphia: Muhlenberg Press, 1961).

36. I tested these themes empirically in "Pace in Learning and Life: Prelude to Pastoral Burnout" (hereafter, "Pace. . ."), and "The Person in Ministry." My (w)holistic questionnaires and scales have now been used with approximately 400 seminarians and 300 pastors. This research is, in part, an effort to study, in the clinical situation, what T. A. Kantonen calls "Christocentric existentialism." Salvatore Maddi, with Suzanne Kobasa, is now working on ways to help caregivers test the related existential themes of challenge, control, and commitment in stressful situations. Cf. S. C. Kobasa and S. R. Maddi, "Existential Personality Theology," in *Current Personality Theories*, R. Corsini, ed. (Itasca, Ill.: Peacock, 1977); Kobasa, Maddi, and S. Kahn, "Hardiness and Health: A Prospective Study," *Journal of Personality and Social Psychology* (1982):42, 168-177; Maddi and Kobasa, *The Hardy Executive: Health Under Stress* (Homewood, Ill.: Dow Jones-Irwin, 1984); and Maya Pines, "Psychological Hardiness: The Role of Challenge in Health," *Psychology Today* 14(7)(1980).

Chapter 2. The Pastor as a Physical Person

37. "Tom's" experience in Hezekiah's tunnel preceded by about five years a report by Karen Hartmann of a somewhat similar situation; cf. "Light At the End of the Tunnel," *The Lutheran Standard*, January 21, 1983. For more on the tunnel in the Old Testament, cf. Bernhard Anderson, pp. 319ff.

38. Harbaugh, "Pace. . .," pp. 81, 98, and "The Person in Ministry," p. 7.

39. *Ibid.* For mitigating factors, cf. Kobasa and Maddi, *The Hardy Executive*, pp. 26-35.

40. Hans Selye first described stress in 1936. Selye's work is best known through such books as *The Stress of Life* (New York: McGraw-Hill, 1956) and *Stress Without Distress* (Philadelphia: Lippincott, 1974). Cf. Keith Sehnert, *Stress/Unstress* (Minneapolis: Augsburg Publishing House, 1981). A good overview of stress research is found in Linus A. Bieliauskas, *Stress and Its Relationship to Health and Illness* (Boulder, Colo.: Westview Press, 1982). Most helpful for me have been the multidisciplinary approaches taken by the Menninger Foundation (Professionals and Their Families workshop, Erwin T. Janssen, director) and the Albert Einstein College of Medicine Institute (Jack F. Wilder and Robert Plutchik, "Professional Burnout: A New Approach to Burnout Prevention"). Wilder and Plutchik reviewed the work of H. Selye, C. Cherniss, J. Edelwich, A.

Brodsky, H. J. Freudenberger, F. Herzberg, M. Kramer, C. Maslach, S. Jackson, A. Pines, E. Aronson, D. Kafry, the Harlem Valley
Psychiatric Center study, among others, and they introduced new
assessment procedures of their own. For a helpful clinical application of stress research in the helping professions, cf. Richard C. W.
Hall, Earl Gardner, Mark Perl, Sondra Stickney, and Betty Pfeffer-
baum, "Professional Burn-out Syndrome," *Psychiatric Opinion*
(4)(April 1979). Janssen (Menninger Foundation, 1981) has
written the helpful guide, "Life Planning—Reviewing the Quality
of Life." Wilder and Plutchik's article, "Preparing the Professional:
Building Prevention into Training," in *Job Stress and Burnout: Research Theory and Intervention Perspectives*, ed. W.S. Paine (Beverly
Hills, Calif.: Sage, 1982) does not specifically address clergy issues,
but it is very relevant to seminary education. Other theologically
oriented materials are cited below.

41. James C. Coleman, *Abnormal Psychology and Modern Life*, 5th ed.
(Glencoe, Ill.: Scott Foresman, 1964, 1976), pp. 109-112.

42. A point emphasized in relation to ordained ministry by Erwin T.
Janssen, Menninger Foundation, "Life Planning. . . ."

43. T. H. Holmes and R. H. Rahe, "The Social Readjustment Rating
Scale," *Journal of Psychosomatic Research* 11 (April 1967):213-218.
Cf. T. H. Holmes and T. S. Holmes, "How Change Can Make Us
Ill," in *Stress* (Blue Cross Association) 25(1)(1974):66ff; the review
of the Holmes-Rahe research in Bieliauskas, "Stress. . .," pp. 45-63,
and B. S. Dohrenwend and B. P. Dohrenwend, eds., *Stressful Life
Events: Their Nature and Effects* (New York: Wiley and Sons, 1974).

44. Harbaugh, "A Model for Caring," p. 22. John M. Schneider reviews
the literature and develops a parallel holistic perspective in his
recent *Stress, Loss, and Grief* (Baltimore: University Park Press,
1984).

45. Gerald Caplan, *Principles of Preventive Psychiatry* (New York: Basic
Books, 1974). On the role of cognitive factors in stress, cf.
Bieliauskas, "Stress. . .," pp. 25ff., R. S. Lazarus, "Cognitive and
Coping Processes in Emotion," in *Stress and Coping: An Anthology*, A.
Monat and Lazarus, eds. (New York: Columbia University Press,
1977).

46. Some recent connections between stress and identity are found in
Alan Reuter, "Stress in the Ministry: Can We Fight Back?" *Currents
in Theology and Ministry*, August, 1981; Donald A. and Nancy Lov-
ing Tubesing, "Stress and Wellness," Care Cassettes, The
American Protestant Hospital Association Series, College of
Chaplains, Chicago, 1981; The Alban Institute research; Charles
A. Rassieur, *Stress Management for Ministers* (Philadelphia: West-
minster Press, 1982); Paul Nicely, "Pastoral Theology of Clergy
Burnout" (Delaware, Ohio: Methodist Theological School), un-
published paper, 1981, and my own materials, "Pace. . .," p. 92 and
"Death: A Theological Reformulation of Developmental and

Existential Perspectives." Note the interrelationship between burnout and the blurring of pastoral identity suggested by Thomas C. Oden, *Pastoral Theology: Essentials of Ministry* (New York: Harper & Row, 1983), pp. 5, 87.

47. Harbaugh, "The Person in Ministry," p. 7. Cf. William E. Hulme, *Your Pastor's Problems* (Garden City, N.Y.: Doubleday, 1966), p. 55. While written some years ago, I find most of Hulme's perceptions in this book to be relevant to current concerns in ordained ministry. Hulme's continued sensitivity is readily apparent in his more recent *Pastoral Care and Counseling* (Minneapolis: Augsburg Publishing House, 1981).

48. The (w)holistic model is meant to illustrate the highly interactive relationship of all the dimensions of our humanness. Cf. Richard Grossman, "The Language of Tension" and "Our Early Warning System," *Family Health*, April and September 1981.

49. Hans Selye, "On the Real Benefits of Eustress," *Psychology Today*, March 1978.

50. Cf. Walter B. Cannon, *The Wisdom of the Body*, 2nd ed. (New York: Norton, 1963).

51. Citing Selye, "Mental Health Quiz," Ohio Department of Mental Health, 1982.

52. Selye, "The General Adaptation Syndrome and the Diseases of Adaptation," *Journal of Clinical Endocrinology*, no. 6(1946), pp. 117-230.

53. Coleman, p. 132.

54. The well-known stages suggested by Elisabeth Kübler-Ross are, in my clinical experience, equally applicable to any situation of significant stress or loss.

55. Einstein seminar (see n. 40).

56. This (w)holistic understanding is based on the anthropology of Martin Buber and Tillich's ontology (the polarity of individuality and participation). Harbaugh, *The Concept of Selfhood in the Theology of Paul Tillich and Its Implications for a Theology of Pastoral Care*, unpublished S.T.M. thesis, Hamma School of Theology, 1967.

57. Coleman, pp. 112ff.

58. Bieliaskus, *Stress*, identifies many psychophysiological reactions to stress (pp. 65-89). Some of these reactions, in my opinion, may well have a hereditary component or be affected by perceptions learned from the family of origin. Theology has seen an individual's history as part of the larger history of the people of God. The psychology of Carl G. Jung has posited a collective unconscious underlying an individual's conscious experience. These are just some of the ways my personal "history" may be understood as larger than my life.

59. The American Lutheran Church and the Lutheran Church in America are currently involved in a "Pastoral Colleague" pilot project with Trinity Lutheran Seminary in the Ohio District/Ohio Synod. William C. Behrens, Paul F. Swartz, Hermann J. Kuhl-

mann, and I comprise the coordinating committee. Bishop K. Bernell Boehm, Connie Sassanella Williams, Robert Wietelmann, and Roy Oswald, Alban Institute, have provided consultation.

60. Nearly 30% of the seminarians surveyed in the Pace Studies acknowledged the use of alcohol or other chemicals to reduce stress (Harbaugh, "Pace. . .," p. 82, and "Pastoral Burnout: A View from the Seminary," with Evan Rogers). Perspectives on substance abuse compatible with my (w)holistic emphasis include Sharon Wegscheider, *Another Chance: Hope and Health for the Alcoholic Family* (Palo Alto: Science and Behavior Books, 1981) and Alan F. Cope, "A Holistic Approach to Alcoholism Treatment," *Trinity Seminary Review* (to be published). Cf. Howard Clinebell, *Understanding and Counseling the Alcoholic*, rev. ed. (Nashville: Abingdon, 1968).

61. Holmes-Rahe assign a maximum 100 life change event units to the death of a spouse (Holmes and Rahe, "Rating Scale").

62. Roy Oswald, *New Beginnings: Pastorate Start-Up Workbook* (Washington, D.C.: Alban Institute), pp. 16-17; cf. Wayne E. Oates, *The Nature of the Minister's Stress* (Care Cassettes, The American Protestant Hospital Association Series, College of Chaplains, Chicago, 1978), and Edgar W. Mills and John P. Koval, *Stress in Ministry* (Washington, D.C.: Ministry Studies Board), 1971.

63. Alan Reuter, p. 222.

64. John J. Gleason Jr., "Perception of Stress Among Clergy and Their Spouses," *Journal of Pastoral Care* 31(4)(December 1977):244ff.

65. Ibid.

66. Coleman, p. 116.

67. Harbaugh, "The Person in Ministry: Psychological Type and the Seminary" (hereafter "Psychological Type/Seminary").

68. This model was presented at clergy seminars in the Chicago area in 1981. Later, I added several additional strategies for coping with stress after seeing the compilation by Reuter, p. 225.

69. Harbaugh, "Pace. . .," pp. 93, 101. The recidivism rates of the Pace Studies were supported by figures reported at the American Psychological Association, Washington, D.C., 1982.

70. G. Lloyd Rediger, *Coping with Clergy Burnout* (Valley Forge: Judson Press, 1982); Roy M. Oswald, *Clergy Burnout* (Alban Institute, Ministers Life Resources, 1982); Rassieur, *Stress*; Reuter, "Stress."

71. Rassieur cites John B. Cobb Jr. as recommending Assagioli's exercise. However, Cobb also had significant reservations (*Theology and Pastoral Care*, p. 22). Cf. Roberto Assagioli, *Psychosynthesis: A Manual of Principles and Techniques* (New York: Viking Press, 1971).

72. Reuter, p. 229.

73. Ibid., p. 230.

74. Harbaugh, "Pace. . .," pp. 82f. and "The Person in Ministry," pp. 9ff. Some of my studies have been influenced by and are consistent with those of Maddi and Kobasa, (see n. 36). In part, I am addressing the theological parallels of hardiness and their implications for

ministry. Also see Paul Tournier, *To Resist or To Surrender* (Richmond: John Knox Press, 1964), pp. 60, 210, and *The Person Reborn* (New York: Harper & Row, 1966), pp. 169f.

75. Hulme, *Pastoral Care and Counseling* (Minneapolis: Augsburg Publishing House, 1981), p. 25.

Chapter 3. The Pastor as a Thinking Person

76. Cf. John Harris, *Stress, Power and the Ministry* (Washington, D.C.: Alban Institute, 1977); "Nobody's Perfect," The Ministers Life & Casualty Union (Minneapolis), which is based on Harris' work; Roy M. Oswald, *Crossing the Boundary* (Washington, D.C.: Alban Institute, 1980), is an important account of research on these transitional years; Mills and Koval, *Stress in Ministry*; the Einstein seminar (see n. 40), especially J. Edelwich and A. Brodsky, *Burn-out: Stages of Disillusionment in the Helping Professions* (New York: Human Sciences Press, 1980) and Christina Maslach, *Burnout—The Cost of Caring* (Englewood Cliffs: Prentice-Hall, 1982). Janet F. Fishburn, Neill Q. Hamilton, and Charles Rice are currently making a major longitudinal study of the first three years of ministry (The Theological School, Drew University, Madison, N.J.), which should prove very valuable in understanding this transitional time. Cf. Fishburn and Hamilton, "Seminary Education Tested by Praxis," *The Christian Century*, February 1-8, 1984.

77. Ibid., esp. Harris and Ministers Life Resources.

78. The Midwest Career Development Services indicate a good to superior level of concept mastery among clergy candidates. Concept mastery is correlated with standard measures of intelligence. Frank C. Williams, director, personal communication.
    u44

79. Cf. Fowler, *Stages of Faith*. Some interesting work in this area is being done by Richard Bradley, Lutheran campus pastor at Ohio State University. Robert Rodgers and Debra Hallock Phillips at OSU have done related studies. Cf. Leland E. Elhard, "Living Faith: Some Contributions of the Concept of Ego-identity to the Understanding of Faith," in Peter A. Homans, ed., *The Dialogue between Theology and Psychology* (Chicago: University of Chicago Press, 1968), pp. 135-162.

80. The Midwest Career Development Service is an excellent program and the one with which I am most familiar. Seminarians and pastors can use the services on an individual or a group basis. Similar services are available in other parts of the country.

81. I am personally biased in favor of the use of psychological testing both prior to and during seminary, and at times of personal or vocational reassessment. However, psychological tests can be misused. Care should be taken to have any testing results reviewed by a competent clinical psychologist in personal interview. It is also

important to remember that no test is adequate to a human being. Tests are partial perspectives on personhood and, understood as such, they can be exceedingly valuable.

82. David Shapiro, *Neurotic Styles* (New York: Basic Books, 1965), p. 18.
83. David A. Kolb has published widely. A good place to begin is with his *Learning Style Inventory Technical Manual*, rev. ed. (Boston: McBer and Co., 1978).
84. For the theoretical framework, cf. Carl G. Jung, *Psychological Types* (Princeton, N.J.: Princeton University Press, 1971, 1977), and for a look at the man behind the theory, Jung's *Memories, Dreams, and Reflections* (New York: Pantheon Books, 1961) and Peter A. Homans, *Jung in Context: Modernity and the Making of a Psychologist* (Chicago: University of Chicago Press, 1979). The fundamentals of the Myers-Briggs Type Indicator are available in a very readable book: Isabel Briggs Myers, with Peter B. Myers, *Gifts Differing* (Palo Alto: Consulting Psychologists Press, 1980, 1983). Trinity Lutheran Seminary routinely administers the MBTI to incoming students.
85. Harbaugh, "Psychological Type/Seminary." The Midwest Career Development Services in 1983 had candidates in 15 of the 16 possible Myers-Briggs type combinations (Frank C. Williams, personal communication) and the Center for Applications of Psychological Type (CAPT) has recorded clergy or church workers in all 16 (Mary H. McCaulley, CAPT).
86. The Person in Ministry research and major findings have been reviewed not only in this country, but also in discussion with Canon Derek Blows, Denis Duncan, and John Foskett (England), James Chamberlain (Ireland), O. K. R. Birkholzer, Hermann Vorlander, Wolfram Fischer, Paul Zulehner, and Hans Schwarz (Germany), Teunis Kruijne, Rein Nauta, Heije Faber, and C. H. Lindijer (The Netherlands), Robert Bendick (Italy), and Rudolph Albisser, Charles Steiner, and Paul Tournier (Switzerland).
87. Canon Derek Blows alerted me to a fine article by Hugh A. Eadie, "The Helping Personality," in *Context: The Interdisciplinary Journal of Pastoral Studies*, no. 49. Most of Eadie's observations parallel my own.
88. Harbaugh, "Psychological Type/Seminary."
89. I am indebted to Bishop Kenneth Sauer, Ohio Synod, Lutheran Church in America, for his helpful perceptions and for referring me to Ralph Underwager's address to pastors, "Stresses of the Ministry and How the Law and Gospel Work," Cassette Tape, Ohio Lutheran Pastor's Conference, 1978. Cf. Hulme, *Your Pastor's Problems*, and J. L. Packer, "Perfectionism: Fraught with Fruits of Self-Destruction," *Christianity Today*, April 10, 1981, pp. 24-27.
90. Cf. Wayne E. Oates, *The Christian Pastor*, pp. 96-127; Milo L. Brekke, Merton P. Strommen, and Dorothy L. Williams, *Ten Faces of Ministry* (Minneapolis: Augsburg Publishing House, 1979); David S. Schuller, M. P. Strommen, M. Brekke, eds., *Ministry in*

America (San Francisco: Harper & Row, 1980); Thomas Kadel, ed., *Growth in Ministry* (Philadelphia: Fortress Press, 1980). One example of a denominational statement is *Expectations of the Lutheran Church in America of Its Ordained Ministers*, [published in *LCA Partners*, October/November 1984 (Philadelphia: Division for Professional Leadership)].

91. "Responsibility," LCA *Expectations . . . .*
92. This is a crucial inference from the research of John Benton Jr., "Perceptual Characteristics of Episcopal Pastors," *Florida Studies in the Helping Professions*, A. Combs, ed. (Gainesville: University of Florida Press, 1969), consistent with my observations in "Pace. . . ." I am grateful to one of my students, Franklin Wester, for leading me to Benton's important research. Cf. Charles F. Kemp, *A Pastoral Triumph* (New York: Macmillan, 1948), p. 93; Hulme (see n. 47), p. 26; and Richard Krebs, "Why Pastors Should Not Be Counselors," *Journal of Pastoral Care*, December 1980, pp. 229-233, Oden, *Pastoral Theology*, pp. 188, 191ff., and a book I have not reviewed but has been recommended to me, Harold C. Warlick Jr., *How to Be a Minister and a Human Being* (Valley Forge, Penn.: Judson Press, 1982). Concern for the pastor as a person is hardly new, as is evident in Wayne E. Oates, ed., *The Minister's Own Mental Health* (Great Neck, N.Y.: Channel Press, 1955).
93. "Not to be ministered unto, but to minister" (KJV), from "Introduction," LCA *Expectations . . . .*
94. Cf. L. Mack Powell, "Ministers and Guilt Problems," *Christian Ministry*, January 1980, pp. 29-30.
95. Cf. William A. Clebsch and Charles R. Jaekle, *Pastoral Care in Historical Perspective* (Englewood Cliffs, N.J.: Prentice-Hall, 1964).
96. The discussion that follows reflects some of the emphases of Donald L. Huber in his review of Clebsch and Jaekle (Trinity Lutheran Seminary, 1981).
97. "Introduction," LCA *Expectations. . . .*
98. Talcott Parsons, "Social Structures . . ." (see n. 24).
99. "The Ordained Minister—Identity" and "Faith and Prayer," LCA *Expectations. . . .* Cf. *A Study of Ministry* (Philadelphia: the Lutheran Church in America, 1980), p. 9.
100. Harbaugh, "The Person in Ministry," p. 8, using Wilder and Plutchik's "Coping Assessment."
101. Taking responsibility for one's own feelings is a basic tenet of assertiveness training. Among secular approaches, I like best that of Patricia Jakubowski and Arthur J. Lange, *Responsible Assertive Behavior: Cognitive/Behavioral Procedures for Trainers* (Champaigne, Ill.: Research Press, 1976), and Colleen Kelley, *Assertion Training: A Facilitator's Guide* (La Jolla, Calif.: University Associates, 1979). Ministry-oriented assertiveness is developed by David W. Augsburger, *Anger and Assertiveness in Pastoral Care* (Philadelphia: Fortress Press, 1979) and Andrew D. Lester, *Coping with Your Anger: A*

Christian Guide (Philadelphia: Westminster Press, 1983). Lester provides a compatible and helpful holistic orientation for his discussion of anger.

102. John Benton Jr., pp. 45f. (see n. 92).
103. Ibid., p. 44.
104. Ibid., p. 46.
105. Ibid., pp. 45f.
106. Ibid.
107. My Person in Ministry studies have been corroborated by the experience of the Midwest Career Development Services (see n. 26), who find maturity and independence the number two counseling issue in candidates (Frank C. Williams, personal communication).
108. Benton, "Perceptual Characteristics . . . ."
109. Ibid.
110. Ibid.
111. Ibid.
112. Ibid. These characteristics are similarly valued by the congregations of the church. Cf. note 90. The Association of Theological Schools' Readiness for Ministry program is also sensitive to these personal and pastoral values.
113. Martin Luther, *Small Catechism*, in Theodore G. Tappert, ed., *The Book of Concord* (Philadelphia: Fortress Press, 1959), p. 352.
114. The Person in Ministry and Pace research is intended to help the church identify how the seminary can better prepare persons for ministry, especially parish ministry. Other efforts to enable growth among pastors include books, e.g. Thomas E. Kadel, ed., *Growth in Ministry*, and such programs as that directed by Peter L. Steinke, Clergy Care System of the Lutheran Social Service, Dallas, Texas.

Chapter 4. The Pastor as a Feeling Person

115. Harbaugh, "Psychological Type/Seminary"; Cf. Mary H. McCaulley, "Type Table: Clergy and Religious Workers," Center for Applications of Psychological Type, Gainesville, Florida.
116. Henri J. M. Nouwen, "Depression in the Seminary," in *Intimacy: Pastoral Psychological Essays* (Notre Dame: Fides Publishers, 1969), pp. 93-119, esp. p. 97.
117. This is a basic principle of assertiveness training. See note 101, Augsburger, *Anger . . .*, p. 4, and Lester, *Coping. . .*, pp. 37ff.
118. L. Mack Powell, pp. 29f. Cf. Arthur H. Becker, *Guilt: Curse or Blessing?* (Minneapolis: Augsburg Publishing House, 1977).
119. Ibid.
120. Harbaugh, "Psychological Type/Seminary."
121. Cf. Anna Freud, *The Ego and the Mechanisms of Defense* (New York: International Universities Press, 1946). The Midwest Career Development Services cites repression of feelings as the number one counseling issue among candidates (Frank C. Williams, personal

communication). Cf. a perspective on feelings that affirms the way women lead men to fuller personhood, Paul Tournier, *The Gift of Feelings* (Richmond: John Knox Press, 1979).

122. Harbaugh, "Psychological Type/Seminary."

123. Ibid. Cf. John Powell, *Why Am I Afraid to Tell You Who I Am?* (Niles, Ill.: Argus Communications, 1969).

124. Cf. Seward Hiltner, *Counselor on Counseling* (Nashville: Abingdon, 1950). Some of the current pastoral counseling resources I find helpful are as follows: C. W. Brister, *The Promise of Counseling* (San Francisco: Harper & Row, 1978), is very good on "presence." I recently learned that Howard Clinebell's *Basic Types of Pastoral Counseling* (Nashville: Abingdon Press, 1966), a standard work, has been completely revised and retitled: *Basic Types of Pastoral Care and Counseling: Resources for the Ministry of Healing and Growth* (1984). He includes his excellent goals from *Growth Counseling* (Nashville: Abingdon, 1979); Wayne E. Oates, *Pastoral Care in Grief and Separation* (Philadelphia: Fortress Press, 1976), makes some important connections in loss situations as do Kenneth R. Mitchell and Herbert Anderson, in *All Our Losses, All Our Griefs* (Philadelphia: Westminster Press, 1983); William E. Hulme, *Pastoral Care and Counseling*, is excellent pastoral theology, and David K. Switzer, *The Minister As Crisis Counselor* (Nashville: Abingdon, 1974), is a careful and comprehensive treatment; William Oglesby Jr., *Biblical Themes in Pastoral Care* (Nashville: Abingdon, 1980), and Donald Capps, op. cit. (see n. 20), and *Biblical Approaches to Pastoral Counseling* (Philadelphia: Westminster, 1981), have provided helpful integrative perspectives.

125. Harbaugh, "Pace . . ." and "The Person in Ministry."

126. Bishops of the Lutheran Church in America and the American Lutheran Church, personal communication. This request is consistent with the research findings of the Association of Theological Schools (see n. 112).

127. Those of us influenced by Kübler-Ross easily made this connection. An early publication of the relevance of Kübler-Ross's stages for the parish was Roy M. Oswald, *The Pastor As Newcomer* (Washington, D.C.: Alban Institute, 1977). Cf. Oswald's *Running Through the Thistles: Terminating a Ministerial Relationship with a Parish* (Washington, D.C.: Alban Institute) and *Pastorate Start Up Workbook*.

128. Franklin Shontz' diagram is compatible with Caplan's theories. I have been unable to locate the source of Shontz's diagram, but cf. *The Psychological Aspects of Physical Illness and Disability* (New York: Macmillan, 1975); Elisabeth Kübler-Ross, *On Death and Dying*; Granger Westberg, *Good Grief* (Philadelphia: Fortress Press, 1971); C. Murray Parkes, *Bereavement* (New York: International Universities Press, 1972); John Bowlby, *Attachment and Loss*, vol. 3 (New York: Basic Books, 1969, 1980); and Erich Lindemann, *Beyond*

Grief (New York: Aronson, 1979), based on his earlier research in the 1940s, which influenced Gerald Caplan. Also see Harbaugh, "A Model for Caring." I recently learned of a parallel approach to grief theorists by John M. Schneider, *Stress, Loss, and Grief.* A further expansion of this model might include the research of Glen W. Davidson, *Living with Dying* (Minneapolis: Augsburg Publishing House, 1975), Davidson, *Understanding Mourning* (Minneapolis: Augsburg, 1984), and a pastoral recasting of the stages, such as done by Carl Nighswonger (see n. 33). For limitations of a stage approach and an alternative, cf. Mitchell and Anderson, *All Our Losses* . . . .

129. One of the continuing critiques of frameworks for understanding such as provided by Kübler-Ross, *et al.*, is the reduction of everyone's experience to a single formula. Having worked with Kübler-Ross, I know how sensitive she was to individual needs and variations in response to death and dying, and I believe the other theorists were aware of these variations as well. Used appropriately by a caring pastor, knowledge of general patterns in grief response can be invaluable. It is wise for a pastor to be aware of literature that helps the clergy appreciate the worldview of special groups. Cf. the discussion of depression in James T. Webb, Elizabeth A. Meckstroth, and Stephanie S. Tolan, *Guiding the Gifted Child* (Columbus, Ohio: Ohio Psychology Publishing Co., 1982), pp. 191-204.

130. Nouwen, *The Wounded Healer: Ministry in Contemporary Society* (New York: Doubleday, 1972), pp. 72f.

131. I have elaborated this theme in "A Model for Caring" and "Death and Identity: Implications for Pastoral Care."

132. Robert Plutchik, *Emotion: A Psychoevolutionary Synthesis* (New York: Harper & Row), 1980; "A Language for the Emotions," *Psychology Today*, February 1980.

133. Ibid., "A Language for the Emotions," p. 74.

134. Plutchik's theories go far beyond what we ordinarily identify as the emotional. His *Emotions Profile Index* has proved very useful in my research among seminarians and pastors. Cf. Robert Plutchik and Henry Kellerman, *Emotions Profile Index* (Los Angeles: Western Psychological Services, 1974).

135. Willard Gaylin, *Feelings: Our Vital Signs* (New York: Harper & Row, 1979), p. 7.

136. Ibid., pp. 7, 11, 17ff.

137. Ibid., p. 12.

138. Ibid., pp. 89ff.

139. Ibid., pp. 12, 165ff.

140. Harbaugh, "Death: A Theological Reformulation of Developmental and Existential Perspectives," and "Death and Identity: Implications for Pastoral Care."

141. Harbaugh, "Pace . . .," p. 93. Cf. Donald Capps, *Pastoral Care: A*

Thematic Approach, p. 144.

142. Cf. Oswald, *The Pastor As Newcomer*, p. 2, and *Running through the Thistles*. The magnitude of the need is evident when we are told that, each year, one congregation out of every three has to work through a pastoral transition (Robert G. Kemper, *Beginning a New Pastorate* [Nashville: Abingdon], 1978).

143. Nouwen, *Wounded Healer*.

144. Ibid., pp. 83ff. Nouwen's chapter, "Ministry by a Lonely Minister," is profound.

145. Ibid., pp. 94f.

146. Ibid., pp. 89f.

147. Ibid., p. 73. The inability to be a "woundless" wounded healer was perceptively pointed out by one of my students.

148. The most provocative and personal development of the relation of life experience to our own death is by Ernest Becker, *The Denial of Death* (New York: The Free Press, 1973). Cf. LeRoy H. Aden, "The Challenge of Becker," *LCA Partners*, August/September 1984.

149. Douglas John Hall, *Lighten Our Darkness: Toward An Indigenous Theology of the Cross* (Philadelphia: Westminster, 1976).

150. Nouwen, *Wounded Healer*, p. 95.

151. Margaretta K. Bowers, *Conflicts of the Clergy* (New York: Thomas Nelson & Sons, 1963), p. 3; Cf. Hulme (see n. 47), pp. 106ff.

152. Nouwen, *Wounded Healer*, p. 89.

153. Ibid.

154. I recommend reading the moving personal reflection on "the winter of the heart" by Martin E. Marty, *A Cry of Absence* (San Francisco: Harper & Row, 1983).

Chapter 5. The Pastor as a Relating Person

155. Coleman, p. 120.

156. While I differ with him in several important areas, the best pastoral resource I know on sexuality and the pastor is Charles Rassieur, *The Problem Clergymen Don't Talk About* (Philadelphia: Westminster, 1976). Rassieur notes that the perspective of the female clergy is also needed.

157. Hulme, *Your Pastor's Problems*, pp. 74f.

158. Dennis C. King and John C. Glidewell, "Power," in *Annual Handbook for Group Facilitators* (University Associates Press, 1976), pp. 139-142. Cf. Hulme, *Two Ways of Caring* (Minneapolis: Augsburg Publishing House, 1973), pp. 69-79. A most enlightening treatment is Richard Sennett's *Authority* (New York: Knopf, 1980).

159. Eric Berne, *Games People Play: The Psychology of Human Relationships* (New York: Grove Press, 1964), esp. the analysis of the adaptive "child," pp. 26f.

160. Sennett, *Authority*, pp. 28, 33ff.

161. Ibid., p. 4.
162. Berne, *Games* . . ., and Sennett, *Authority*.
163. Harbaugh, "The Person in Ministry," p. 7. Cf. note 107.
164. Elisabeth O'Conner, *The New Community* (New York: Harper & Row), pp. 57ff.
165. Cf. Samuel Southard, *Anger in Love* (Philadelphia: Westminster, 1973); Norman Rohrer and S. Philip Sutherland, *Facing Anger: How to Turn Life's Most Troublesome Emotion into a Personal Asset* (Minneapolis: Augsburg Publishing House, 1981); Richard A. Donnenwirth and Henry B. Marksbury, "Effective Coping with Anger," Care Cassettes, The American Protestant Hospital Association Series, College of Chaplains, Chicago, 1979.
166. This is another basic tenet of assertiveness training. See note 101.
167. King and Glidewell, p. 139, quoting R. M. Emerson, "Power Dependence Relations," *American Sociological Review* 27(1962):31-41.
168. It is helpful to consider dependence–independence in relation to self-actualization. Cf. Abraham H. Maslow, "Deficiency Motivation and Growth Motivation," in M. R. Jones, ed., *Nebraska Symposium on Motivation* (Lincoln: University of Nebraska Press, 1955), and "Some Basic Propositions of a Growth and Self-Actualization Psychology," in *Perceiving, Behaving, Becoming: A New Focus for Education* (Washington, D.C.: Yearbook of the Association for Supervision and Curriculum Development, 1962).
169. Rebecca E. Hight, "Burnout," *Christian Ministry* 11(November 1980):31-33.
170. Tillich, *Theology*, vol. 3, p. 43.
171. I have used this model in course work on Sexuality and Relationship Counseling. Recently I added additional factors based on the research of Ruth G. Sherman, "Typology and Problems in Intimate Relationships," *Research in Psychological Type*, vol. 4, Thomas G. Carskadon, ed. (Mississippi State University, 1981), pp. 4-23.
172. Harold Fishbein, M.D., Ohio Academy of Family Physicians Continuing Education Project in Psychiatry, Springfield, Ohio, 1977.
173. Cf. note 32. Pastoral counselors will also want to become familiar with Douglas Anderson, *New Approaches to Family Pastoral Care* (Philadelphia: Fortress, 1980), and Herbert Anderson, *The Family and Pastoral Care* (Philadelphia: Fortress, 1984).
174. Cf. David and Vera Mace, *What's Happening to Clergy Marriages* (Nashville: Abingdon, 1980), Harbaugh and William C. Behrens, "The Pastor's Spouse," *Trinity Seminary Review*, Fall 1984.
175. Harbaugh, "Psychological Type/Seminary." Cf. Center for Applications of Personality Type table for Clergy and Religious Workers, Mary H. McCaulley (see n. 115).
176. David Keirsey and Marilyn Bates, *Please Understand Me: Character and Temperament Types*, 3rd ed. (Del Mar, Calif.: Prometheus Nemesis Books, 1978), pp. 30-39, 67ff. Cf. Isabel Briggs Myers (see nn. 84, 232), pp. 127-135.

177. Sherman, p. 14.
178. Ibid., p. 15 and McCaulley, personal communication.
179. Sherman, pp. 14ff.
180. On the contrary, a study of pastors showed clergy considered "effective" by their bishops typically worked 60 or more hours a week. Cf. Allan H. Sager, "Frequently Noted Characteristics of Effective Pastors," *Trinity Seminary Review* 4(2)(Fall 1982). But note Martin Luther's admonition: "Do not overwork 'for the glory of God,' " in Ewald M. Plass, ed., *What Luther Says* (St. Louis: Concordia Publishing House, 1959), p. 787.
181. An example is provided by the Ohio Synod, L.C.A., and the Ohio District, A.L.C., using Growth in Ministry materials of the Lutheran Church. Mace and Mace (see n. 174) also point out the importance of innovative programs for pastors and their spouses, pp. 131f. A recent study by David J. Rolfe and Danielle C. Mahrer identifies *The Marriage Preparation, Enrichment, and Counseling Services Provided by Seminaries and Judicatories for Lutheran and Anglican Clergy Families in North America* (Spokane: Lutheran Social Services of Washington, 1984).
182. Bishop Royall Yount of the Florida Synod, Lutheran Church in America, offered helpful comments about pastors' needs. To support consultation apart from the bishop's office, he has identified professional resource persons throughout Florida to whom pastors can go with complete anonymity and Synod support.
183. Sennett, *Authority*, p. 18.
184. Ted Daugherty, "Pastoral Authority and Identity," Care Cassettes, The American Hospital Association Series, College of Chaplains, Chicago, 1976.
185. Hulme, *Your Pastor's Problems*, pp. 72f.
186. The Alban Institute, Washington, D.C., has published and/or leads workshops in pastoral power and authority issues. Cf. Harris, *Stress, Power and the Ministry*, and the work of Speed Leas. Also, cf. Speed Leas and Paul Kitlaus, *Church Fights: Managing Conflict in the Local Church* (Philadelphia: Westminster, 1973).
187. John Fletcher, *Religious Authenticity in the Clergy* (Washington, D.C.: Alban Institute). There are a number of "stage" theories relating to clergy. One very interesting approach to pastoral counseling, which is also relevant to entrance into a parish, is Robert L. Randall, "Stages in the Role Cycle of Pastoral Counseling," *Journal of Pastoral Care* 76(2)(1982). The theme of a recent interview of Roy M. Oswald is suggestive (Oswald, "Pastoral Passages," in *Leadership* [Fall Quarter 1983]).
188. Fletcher, *Religious Authenticity.*
189. Ibid.
190. Paul A. Mickey and Robert L. Wilson, *Conflict and Resolution* (Nashville: Abingdon, 1973), p. 9.
191. Harbaugh, "Psychological Type/Seminary."

192. Ibid.
193. Mickey and Wilson, *Conflict and Resolution*, p. 17.
194. Fletcher, *Religious Authenticity in the Clergy*.
195. Ibid.

Chapter 6. The Pastor as a Choosing Person

196. Cf. T. A. Kantonen, *The Theology of Evangelism* (Philadelphia: Muhlenberg Press, 1954), p. 17.
197. Ronald M. Hals helps us see the continuity between the Old and New Testaments through his discussion of "God's Gracious Choices," in *Grace and Faith in the Old Testament* (Minneapolis: Augsburg Publishing House, 1980), pp. 21-32.
198. Reuel L. Howe, *The Miracle of Dialogue* (Greenwich, Conn.: Seabury Press, 1963).
199. William A. Miller, "Self Image: How Come and How To," Care Cassettes, the American Protestant Hospital Association Series, College of Chaplains, Chicago, 1978. I have just recently learned of the work of M. Scott Peck. See especially his chapters on risk and grace in *The Road Less Traveled* (New York: Simon and Schuster, 1978).
200. Cf. Wayne E. Oates, *Confessions of a Workaholic* (Nashville: Abingdon, 1971).
201. Tillich, *The Courage to Be* (New Haven: Yale University Press, 1953).
202. Caplan, *Principles of Preventive Psychiatry*.
203. I believe this underlies Maddi's and Kosaba's perspective on stress and hardiness. Cf. the article by Maddi, Kobasa, and R. R. J. Hilker summarized in Pines, *Psychology Today*, and *The Hardy Executive* (n. 36). Also see my development of "faith-hardiness" in "Change and the Hardy Pastor," *LCA Partners* (the professional leadership magazine of the Lutheran Church in America), December/January 1984. William C. Behrens, Office of Support to Ministries, the American Lutheran Church, and I have tested out "faith-hardiness" in work-shops for pastors and spouses in mid-life and long-term ministries. I am currently writing on how Christians can grow in faith-hardiness in *The Faith-Hardy Christian* (forthcoming from Augsburg Publishing House).
204. Harbaugh, "Psychological Type/Seminary."
205. Cf. C. S. Lewis, *The Problem of Pain* (New York: Macmillan, 1945), and Paul Tournier, ed., *Fatigue in Modern Society* (Richmond: John Knox Press, 1945), pp. 8-34.
206. Harbaugh, "Perceptual and Value Differences Between the Terminally Ill and the Physically Healthy," unpublished research project, University of Chicago, 1968.
207. Ibid.
208. Boisen, *Out of the Depths* (New York: Harper), 1960; Harry Stack

Sullivan, *The Interpersonal Theory of Psychiatry*, and Karl Jaspers, *Man and the Modern Age*, trans. Eden and Cedar Paul (London: Routledge and K. Paul, 1951).

209. Harbaugh, "Perceptual and Value Differences . . . ." (In this study, statistical significance was determined at a probability of .05 or less.)

210. Cf. "A Study of Ministry, 1984," review draft, Division for Professional Leadership, Lutheran Church in America, July 1983.

211. "Expectations . . .," LCA, p. 1. In a study of supervisors and seminary interns, Russell F. Seabright found that they rated "enabling lay ministry" only seventh or eighth important among eleven ministry functions. Cf. Seabright, "Developing a Model of Supervision for the Integration of Social Awareness," D.Min. Project, United Theological Seminary, Dayton, Ohio, 1984. Constructive approaches to the enabling of lay ministry include Diane Detwiler-Zapp and William Caveness Dixon, *Lay Caregiving* (Philadelphia: Fortress Press, 1982), and Arthur H. Becker's *The Compassionate Visitor: Resources for Ministering to People Who Are Ill* (Minneapolis: Augsburg Publishing House, 1984). I also like Hulme's chapter on the congregation in *Pastoral Care and Counseling*.

212. Caplan, *Principles of Preventive Psychiatry*.

213. Cf. Marty, *A Cry of Absence*, p. 45.

214. During a Clinical Ministry sequence with Carl Nighswonger and Murray Ford, I was made even more aware of the dynamics during the valley experiences of life. Cf. Nighswonger (see n. 33). Cf. Marty, *Cry* . . ., pp. 158ff.

215. Tillich, *Systematic Theology*, vols. 1-3 (esp. vol. 3).

216. Harbaugh, "Death and Identity: Implications for Pastoral Care."

217. Harbaugh, "Death: A Theological Reformulation of Developmental and Existential Perspectives."

218. Ibid. Cf. Daniel Day Williams, *The Minister and the Care of Souls*, p. 29.

219. This was during my tenure as Director of Emergency Services at the Brevard County Community Mental Health Center, Rockledge, Florida, where I served in various clinical capacities between 1972-76.

220. While I have not attended their workshops, I understand this is one of the goals of Dennis and Matthew Linn. Cf. *Healing Life's Hurts: Healing Memories through the Five Stages of Forgiveness* (New York: Paulist Press, 1978).

221. The resources I consider to be the most helpful in support of this kind of ministry are listed in note 124.

222. Ronald Hals notes that the Hebrew word for salvation is *Yasha'*, which is derived from a root meaning "to be wide or spacious or to make wide." One of my students, David Delaney, brought this to my attention after hearing the story of Hezekiah's tunnel. Cf. Marty, *Cry* . . ., pp. 123, 170.

223. T. A. Kantonen on Luther. Cf. Ewald M. Plass, *What Luther Says* (St. Louis: Concordia Publishing House, 1959), p. 734.

224. Joseph Sittler, *The Ecology of Faith*, pp. 97f.

225. Cf. Kenneth R. Pelletier, *Holistic Medicine: From Stress to Optimum Health* (New York: Delacorte Press, 1979), and Herbert Benson with Miriam Z. Klipper, *The Relaxation Response* (New York: Avon Books, 1975).

226. Drs. Richard and Darlene Truchses, Vail, Colorado, who since that time have provided periodic workshops for clergy in stress management.

227. Nouwen, *Creative Ministry* (Garden City, N.Y.: Doubleday, 1971), p. 51. Cf. Donald A. and Nancy Loving Tubesing, *The Caring Question* (Minneapolis: Augsburg Publishing House, 1983).

228. Elliott W. Schilke, M.D., introduced me to the relaxation exercises of Edmund Jacobson, *Progressive Relaxation* (Chicago: University of Chicago Press, 1938).

229. Paul Tournier, *The Meaning of Persons* (New York: Harper & Row, 1956), pp. 106ff., and *The Whole Person in a Broken World*. The integration of relaxation and prayer that follows, written for a lay audience, appeared as "Praying Stress Away," *The Lutheran*, July, 1984. Herbert Benson has recently seen the value of such integration. Cf. Daniel Goleman, "The Faith Factor," *American Health*, May 1984, based on Benson's newest work, *Beyond the Relaxation Response* (New York: Times Books, 1984).

230. In addition to *Gifts Differing*, cf. Mary H. McCaulley, *Jung's Theory of Psychological Types and the Myers-Briggs Type Indicator* (Gainesville: Center for Applications of Psychological Type, 1981), Gordon Lawrence, *People Types and Tiger Stripes: A Practical Guide to Learning Styles*, 2nd ed. (Gainesville: CAPT, 1982), and Carl G. Jung, *Psychological Types*.

231. I am now preparing for publication the results of interdenominational and interdisciplinary research I have done with the support of the Association of Theological Schools and the Commission on Interprofessional Education and Practice, Ohio State University, which will appear as *The Helping Person* (Gainesville: CAPT).

232. Cf. Isabel Briggs Myers, *Gifts Differing*.

233. Cf. John Ackerman, "Cherishing Our Differences" (Pecos, N.M.: Dove Publications); W. Harold Grant, Magdala Thompson, Thomas E. Clarke, *From Image to Likeness: A Jungian Path in the Gospel Journey* (New York: Paulist Press, 1983); and the very helpful *Finding and Following Your Spiritual Path* by Earle C. Page (Gainesville, Fla.: Center for Applications of Psychological Type, 1982). Roy Oswald of the Alban Institute has also been exploring this area (personal communication).

234. Lee Griffin, a psychiatrist and longtime consultant with the American Lutheran Church, recently commented on his increasing sensitivity to the effect of very early life experiences (personal com-

munication). O'Connell and O'Connell, *Choice and Change*, note the importance of letting go of the past, p. 53.

235. Alan Sager, who has trained in the Progoff method, recently completed with good results an experimental course in journaling at Trinity Lutheran Seminary. Cf. Ira Progoff, *At a Journal Workshop* (New York: Dialog House Library, 1975).

236. Matthew Fox, *On Being a Musical Mystical Bear* (New York: Paulist Press, 1972); cf. *Spirituality: Aspects of Christian Life and Renewal* (Division for Life and Mission in the Congregation, the American Lutheran Church, 1980). Something of this spirit is caught by Robert L. Randall's title, *Holy Wholeness* (to be published) and by John Carmody, *Holistic Spirituality* (New York: Paulist, 1983). My research over the past five years has led me to an ever-increasing awareness of the need for seminaries to help prospective pastors not only learn theology but also mature spiritually. In every one of the (w)holistic studies, a pastor's ability to "see with the eyes of faith" is consistently and significantly correlated with effective and faithful ministry. This theme is developed in my most recent reflection on fragmentation, integration, and spirituality, "Preparing the Person for Ministry: Three Challenges," *The Future of Seminary Education in the Lutheran Church: Trinity Lutheran Seminary Review*, special edition, Columbus, Ohio, 1984.